The Olivet Discourse
Christ Speaks of His Second Coming

Don T. Phillips

"The Olivet Discourse: Christ Speaks of His Second Coming," by Don T. Phillips. ISBN 978-1-63868-171-7.

Published 2024 by Virtualbookworm.com Publishing Inc., P.O. Box 9949, College Station, TX 77845, US. Copyright ©2024 Don T. Phillips.

All rights reserved. No part of this publication may be reproduced, stored in a retrieval system, or transmitted in any form or by any means, electronic, mechanical, recording or otherwise, without the prior written permission of Don T. Phillips.

Table of Contents

Chapter 1: Winds of Change 1

Chapter 2: When Will the Temple be Destroyed? 8
   The Siege of Jerusalem in 70 AD 12

Chapter 3: When Shall These Things Be? 15
   The Seven Seals: Traditional Chronology 23
   The Seven Seals: Correct Chronology 26

Chapter 4: The Great Tribulation Begins 54

Chapter 5: What Will Be the Sign of Thy Coming? 68
   The Parable of the Fig Tree 68

Chapter 6: Parable of the Wise and Foolish Virgins 82

Chapter 7: The Parable of the Talents 102

Chapter 8: The Judgment of the Nations 116
   The Seven Dispensations of Time 125

EPILOG 134

Bibliography 136

Preface

Jesus Christ had come to Jerusalem for the Feast of Passover. It would be the last week of His earthly Ministry. Christ would be examined and questioned every day in Herod's Temple as he taught and healed all who would come to him. Christ was the perfect Passover Lamb who was examined every day by the Scribes, Sadducees and Pharisees who sought to find a fault or blemish… but there was none.

As Jesus departed the temple and the City of Jerusalem for the last time as a free man, He turned to His disciples and said: *See ye not all these things? verily I say unto you: There shall not be left here one stone upon another, that shall not be thrown down* (Matthew 24:2). His disciples were stunned. This was Herod's Temple, which had stood for almost 50 years and was more than just a building, it was the heart of Jewish religion and the most sacred building in Jerusalem. The disciples followed Jesus in silence across the Kidron Valley and up the Mt. of Olives where they all gathered to hear Christ. As they all began to sit down: Peter, James, John, and Andrew (Mark 13:3) came to Him privately and posed the following questions.

The East Gate of Jerusalem. It was sealed in 1541 AD

Tell us, when shall these things be? and what shall be the sign of thy coming, and of the end of the world?   Matthew 24:3

The response which Jesus Christ gave to these questions has become known as the *Olivet Discourse*. It is the longest and most comprehensive discussion of the 2nd Coming of Jesus Christ that is contained in the synoptic gospels. It is the last of *Five Discourses* which appear in the Book of Matthew: The *Sermon on the Mount*, the *Mission Discourse*, the *Parabolic Discourse*, the *Discourse on the Church,* and the *Discourse of His 2nd Advent* and the *End Times.* This book is a complete discussion of the 5th Discourse. Parallel records can be found in Mark 13, and Luke 21. The most

The Siege and Destruction of Jerusalem, by David Roberts **(1850)**

comprehensive record of the Olivet Discourse is in Matthew 24-25, parallel records can be found in Mark 13, and Luke 21. A general outline of the Olivet Discourse is as follows.

- There will be wars and rumors of wars.
- Jesus then identifies the *beginning of birth pains*
    - Nations rising up against nations, and kingdoms against kingdoms
    - Earthquakes
    - Famines
    - Pestilence
    - Fearful events.

Jesus next described widespread persecution which would lead to His 2nd coming

- False prophets
- Apostasy
- Persecution of the followers of Jesus;
- Spread of the Gospel message throughout the world.
- The abomination of desolation standing in the Temple

After Jesus described the *abomination that causes desolation*, He warns that the people of Judea should flee to the mountains as a matter of such urgency that they shouldn't even return to get things from their homes. Jesus also warned that if it happened in winter or on a Sabbath Day, fleeing would be even more difficult. Jesus described this as a time of *Great Tribulation* worse than anything that had ever gone before.

Jesus then revealed that *immediately after* the time of *Great Tribulation* people would see a sign: *the sun will be darkened, and the moon will not give its light; the stars will fall from the sky, and the heavenly bodies will be shaken.*

The Sun and Moon turning dark are unprecedented, but are prophesied in the Book of Isaiah (Joel 3:15). The Book of Revelation mentions the Sun and Moon turning dark during the opening of the 6th Seal.

Jesus states that after the time of tribulation and the sign of the Sun, Moon, and stars going dark the Son of Man would be seen arriving in the clouds with power and great glory. The Son of Man would be accompanied by the angels and at the trumpet call the angels would gather his elect from the four winds, from one end of heaven to the other (Matthew 24:31). This undoubtedly is a reference to what we call the *Rapture*.

At this point, Jesus began to speak to His disciples in Parables. Three Parables were spoken concerning the 2nd advent of Jesus Christ.

- The *Parable of the Fig Tree*... Matthew 24:3
- The *Parable of the Wise and Foolish Virgins*... Matthew 25: 1-13
- The *Parable of the Talents*... Matthew 25: 14-30

The Olivet Discourse concludes with a prophecy of a judgment which will take place after the Church Age is over following the Battle of Armageddon.

- The *Judgment of the Nations*, or the *Judgment of the Sheep and Goats*... Matthew 25: 31-46

This book will discuss in detail all of the words spoken by Jesus Christ in the Olivet Discourse (Matthew 24-Matthew 25).

Chapter 1…... Winds of Change

Chapter 2...... When will the Temple be Destroyed?
Chapter 3...... When Shall These Things Be?
Chapter 4...... The Great Tribulation Begins
Chapter 5...... What Will Be the Sign of Thy Coming?
                The Parable of the Fig Tree
Chapter 6...... The Parable of Wise and Foolish Virgins
Chapter 7...... The Parable of the Talents
Chapter 8...... Judgment of The Sheep and Goats
                EPILOG

The Olivet Discourse is the most extensive prophecy in both the Old Testament and the New Testament excluding the Book of Revelation.

Dr. Don T. Phillips
Spring, 2024

Chapter 1
Winds of Change

The time was drawing near that Jesus Christ would be arrested, tried and crucified as a common criminal on the Cross of Calvary. The Jews had been the chosen people of God from the time that Abram (Abraham) was called from Ur of the Chaldees to spawn anew nation called Israel.

[1] Now the LORD had said unto Abram, Get thee out of thy country, and from thy kindred, and from thy father's house, unto a land that I will shew thee:
[2] And I will make of thee a great nation, and I will bless thee, and make thy name great; and thou shalt be a blessing:
*[3] And I will bless them that bless thee, and curse him that curse thee: and in thee shall **all families of the earth be blessed***   Genesis 12: 1-3

The Apostle Paul made it clear that the seed of Abraham that would bless all nations is *Christ.*

And if ye be Christ's, then are ye Abraham's seed, and heirs according to the promise.   Galatians 3:29

In the Old Testament, Jesus Christ and the entire *New Covenant* was completely hidden. Paul called this a *Great Mystery*. The *Old Covenant* and salvation were a Theocracy governed by the Laws of God which God gave to His chosen people, Israel, at Mt. Sinai. The Law regulated almost every aspect of life in Old Testament. Many of the laws were specific for spiritual life, others governed the system of worship and the agricultural life of ancient Israel (Exodus 12:14-16, Leviticus 1:10-13, 11: 1-23, 15: 19-20, 19:19, 19: 27-28, 27: 30-32, Deuteronomy 25: 5-6). God instructed Israel to obey all of the laws which He would give them, and he promised that if they would observe His laws they would be blessed, and they would be cursed if they did not. In a real sense, the law was a curse but it was a blessing. It taught Israel two important truths: (1) The law was good because it was Given by God but (2) The Law was imperfect since no one could live under the law, and sin was by definition breaking the laws of God.

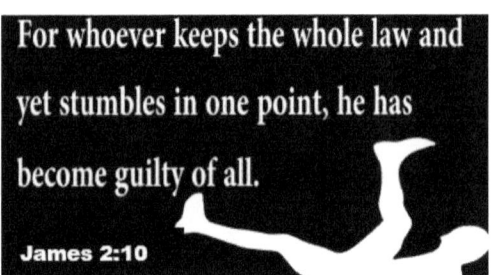

James said that if anyone broke only one command that God gave Israel, the entire law had been broken. The law did not save anyone, it condemned everyone. *Why would God do such a thing?* The Law was not meant to save, but rather to teach all men that it is not possible to live without violating at least one law, and realizing that salvation under the law came to each individual in exactly the same way that it did under the New Covenant…by *faith.* As we examine the Old Testament, there is not even a hint that Jesus Christ would be sent by God to redeem all men from sin. However, there are numerous passages of scripture written by the prophets that a redeemer would one day arise who would save Israel.

If anyone died without the faith that a redeemer would someday be sent from God and offer salvation, they died in sin and will be judged at the *Great White Throne Judgment.* Those who died in the Faith of Abraham that a *seed* of Abraham would one day arise and redeem all Israel…all who would believe in faith… would be saved. Christ came not to destroy the law, but to fulfil the law (Matthew 5:17). He was a sinless savior who died and freed all people from the curse of the law.

[22] *Knowing that a man is not justified by the works of the law, but by the faith of Jesus Christ, even we have believed in Jesus Christ, that we might be justified by the faith of Christ, and not by the works of the law: for by the works of the law shall no flesh be justified.*   Galatians 2:16
[23] *But before faith came, we were kept under the law, shut up unto the faith which should afterwards be revealed.*
[24] *Wherefore the law was our schoolmaster to bring us unto Christ, that we might be justified by faith.*   Galatians 3:23-24

The Old Covenant was about to come to an end. Within 48 hours Jesus Christ was to be Crucified for the sins of the world…past, present and future. Sin would no longer hold the Old Testament Jews captive, but all who believed would be justified by faith. It must be understood that Jesus Christ spoke to the Jews for 3.5 years, and He was terminating condemnation under the law. It is evident that that most Jews and the Jewish religious leaders did not accept Jesus Christ as their long-awaited Messiah. However, his apostles and disciples all recognized that Jesus Christ was the Son of God and that He was the one they had waited on for so long. Under the New Covenant, salvation was by faith alone. Salvation offered to Jews and Gentiles alike was probably poorly understood if at all by the apostles and disciples. It was not until Jesus Christ chose Saul of Tarsus (Paul) to reveal and define the *mystery* of the New Covenant through his preaching, teaching and 12 epistles, that this truth was fully understood. Recall that Paul had been evangelizing in Syria, Turkey and Greece, when he was forced to return to Jerusalem to convince Peter, James and the other disciples that salvation had come to Jews and Gentiles alike (Galatians 1: 1-24). The confrontation that Paul had with Peter and James came about 3 years after he had been chosen by Christ and had spent some time preparing for his ministry in Arabia and Damascus (Galatians 1: 17-18).

Jerusalem on the Left and The Mt. Of Olives on the Right

The disciples were probably dazed and confused as they left Jerusalem, crossed the Kidron Valley, and sat upon the Mount of Olives with their Lord and savior. They undoubtedly expected that Christ would destroy all of their enemies, eradicate Rome and the Roman empire, and establish His earthly reign on His throne of Glory with a resurrected King David. They were in for a great surprise.

Jesus Christ is about to be arrested and sentenced to death by crucifixion. It is less than 36 hours before He must meet His destiny on the Cross of Calvary where the Lamb of God will be crucified for the sins of the world. He has just finished preaching, healing and teaching in Herod's Temple as was His custom during the last week of His ministry here on earth. He and His disciples depart the temple and are about to leave Jerusalem by the east gate. According to Jewish tradition, the Shekhinah Glory (שכינה or Divine Presence) would appear each morning and enter Jerusalem and Herod's Temple through the East gate of the city. Jewish tradition also holds that when their long-awaited Messiah will appear to save all Israel that he would enter Jerusalem through the East gate (Ezekiel 44:1–3). As Jesus was leaving the temple with His disciples, they were all admiring the majesty and size of the Temple.

> And Jesus went out, and departed from the temple: and his disciples came to him for to shew him the buildings of the temple
> Matthew 24:1

Herod's Temple was the holiest structure in all of Israel. The Holy Temple in Jerusalem was never simply a building or an ordinary structure, but it was an earthly dwelling place for the Divine Presence of God (Ezekiel 43:7). The 1st permanent temple was constructed by King Solomon as a place where God would descend to earth and commune with man. It was destroyed by the Babylonian Empire and Nebuchadnezzar in 586 BC. This temple was partially restored by Ezra after 70 years of captivity in Babylon. The 2nd Temple was constructed in the first century BC under the reign of Herod the Great. Hence, it became known as *Herod's Temple*. The temple's reconstruction resulted in a grand and imposing structure. It was built on what is called the *Temple Mount*, where the Islamic *Dome of the Rock* stands today.

Herod began construction of this magnificent temple in 20/19 BC, during the 18th year of his reign. The main construction phase was completed within about a decade. Detailed descriptions of the temple exist in Josephus (*Jewish Antiquities* 15.380–425, *Jewish War* 5.184–247) and in early rabbinic writings. The temple was 172 feet long, 172 feet wide, and 130-140 feet high. It contained the Holy Place where sacrifices were made, the Holy-of-Holies which contained the Ark of the Covenant, and living quarters for the Levite priests. The gates were made of solid brass and the floor of the Holy Place and the Holy-of-Holies was marble. The Holy Place of the ancient *tabernacle* was open, and the Holy-of-Holies of Moses Tabernacle was covered with badger skin. The covering of this area in Herod's Temple is not recorded, but it was said that the height of the temple reached in places to 180 feet. Herod's Temple was one of the largest religious sanctuaries in the ancient world.

As Jesus departed Herod's Temple for the last time during His earthly ministry, the disciples came to Jesus and commented on the magnificent structure, He then turned and made a startling prophecy.

> *See ye not all these things? verily I say unto you, there shall not be left here one stone upon another, that shall not be thrown down*
> Matthew 24:2

The disciples must have been stunned. Jesus had just revealed that the central point of Jewish worship and the most holy place in all of Judea would be totally destroyed. The destruction would be so devastating that there *would not be a single stone that would not be thrown down*. What! The place where God came and visited man in the Holy of Holies once a year on the Day of Atonement would be totally dismantled and destroyed!! No wonder the disciples were stunned. They had probably thought and anticipated that at that time Jesus Christ would not be crucified, but that He would assume His rightful place as King of Kings and Lord of Lords on the rebuilt throne of King David in Herod's

Temple. As Jesus and His disciples left Jerusalem, crossed the Kidron Valley and arrived on the Mt. of Olives their minds must have been spinning. It is likely that Christ stopped and sat down in the Garden of Gethsemane. It was His favorite place to be with His disciples on the Mt. of Olives, and it was here that He would be arrested around Midnight on Nisan 14 to be tried and executed.

Jerusalem on the Left and The Mt. Of Olives on the Right

> *And as he sat upon the mount of Olives, the disciples came unto him privately, saying: Tell us, when shall these things be? and what shall be the sign of thy coming, and of the end of the world?*   Matthew 24:3

The apostles and probably a few of His disciples gathered around Him on the evening of Nisan 13. Full of confusion and concern, they asked Him three questions: (1) When will Herod's Temple be destroyed? (2) What signs should they look for when He comes again? and (3) What signs would herald the end of the world? An alternate translation of the 3rd question is: *What signs would herald the end of the age*? It should be understood that the disciples fully expected that when Jesus Christ comes again this will result in the end of the world. As we explain and examine these three questions, it will become obvious that Christ revealed little concerning Question #1: *When will Herod's Temple be destroyed?* Note that Jesus is speaking to His disciples, and by extension to all Jews. Although He spoke only to Jews, we as Christians will also learn from His response to all three questions. Not only do we have the advantage of hindsight, but we also have the Book of Revelation which was written by the Apostle John around 90 AD - 96 AD. It will be shown that there is a remarkable correlation between the *Olivet Discourse* and the *Book of Revelation*.

The truth which must be fully understood is that when Jesus was healing, preaching and teaching during His 3.5 years of ministry, He was preaching to the Jews, not the Gentiles (Matthew 10:5, Matthew 15: 22-

24). He was born a Jew, lived as a Jew and died as a Jew. The Olivet Discourse was spoken primarily to the Apostles of Christ as they sat upon the Mt. of Olives. It is composed of two main themes. The **1st** is a discourse which describes the second advent of Jesus Christ. The **2nd** is a series of Parables which reveal how the Jews will be judged and redeemed when Christ returns again. It should be recognized that the Church age and salvation to the Gentiles was completely unknown until the Apostle Paul was chosen by God to reveal that salvation under the New Covenant was by *faith,* and that it would be offered to both Jews and Gentiles.

Although seldom recognized by most Christians today, the Olivet Discourse was not spoken to Gentiles, but was given only to the Jews. The concept of a *Great Tribulation*, the rapture of all living saints, the resurrection of all saints who had died, and the 1000-year Millennial Kingdom was not known until Paul revealed the rapture and John wrote the Book of Revelation to all New Covenant believers. The words spoken by Jesus Christ as He described the Great Tribulation and His 2nd advent must not be conflict with those words written by John in the Book of Revelation.

The parables spoken by Jesus Christ are quite different. *The Parable of the Wise and Foolish Virgins* reveal how each Jew and Christian needs to be ready for the Rapture, and the *Parable of the Talents* teach what Christ expects His *Ecclesia* to be doing when He returns again. The last thing revealed by Christ was the *Judgment of the Sheep and Goats* Judgment of the Nations). This judgment was to determine who would join the 12 tribes of Israel in the 1000-Year millennial Kingdom.

The Olivet discourse was recorded in Matthew (Matthew 24:1 - Matthew 25:46), Mark (Mark 13: 1-37) and Luke (Luke 21: 5-38). The narrative recorded by Matthew is the most complete and extensive of the three, and we will use it in this book with occasional reference to Mark and Luke.

Chapter 2
When will the Temple be Destroyed?

This was the 1st question that the apostles asked Jesus. The response which Jesus gave to this question was not specific or revealing, but Jesus Christ had left the Temple for the last time, and when He did the *Chicana Glory* had also departed.
As He left the temple, He declared it to be empty and desolate as far as God was concerned.

[33] *Ye serpents, ye generation of vipers, how can ye escape the damnation of hell?*
[34] *Wherefore, behold, I send unto you prophets, and wise men, and scribes: and some of them ye shall kill and crucify; and some of them shall ye scourge in your synagogues, and persecute them from city to city:*
[35] *That upon you may come all the righteous blood shed upon the earth, from the blood of righteous Abel unto the blood of Zacharias son of Barachias, whom ye slew between the temple and the altar*
Matthew 38: 33-35

*Behold, your house is left unto you **desolate**: and verily I say unto you, Ye shall not see me, until the time come when ye shall say, Blessed is he that cometh in the name of the Lord*   Luke 13:35

This last day in the Temple would be the last public appearance and teaching that Christ would give. From this point on, He would spend His time only with His apostles and His closest disciples. It is also the last departure that Christ would make from the City of Jerusalem as a free man.

The Jews had no excuse for not accepting Jesus Christ as their long-awaited Messiah. It is estimated that Christ fulfilled at least 300 Old Testament prophecies. They knew this, and yet they denied that He was their Messiah sent from God to redeem them from sin. God sent them prophets, but they would not hear them and they killed them for things that they did not understand and would not accept. Christ lamented over them when He left the temple for the last time.

[37] *O Jerusalem, Jerusalem, thou that killed the prophets, and stoned them which are sent unto thee, how often would I have gathered thy children together, even as a hen gathers her chickens under her wings, and ye would not!*
[38] *Behold, your house is left unto you desolate.*   Luke 13: 37-38

This same condemnation upon Herod, the Jewish spiritual leadership and the Holy Temple is found in Matthew 23:38. In Matthew 23 Jesus is leaving the temple for the last time, but in Luke 13: 35-38 He is in Galilee. Christ said that they would not see Him until He came again. *What did He mean by this statement?* They saw Him when He was arrested and condemned to die.... they saw Him as He was dragged through the streets of the Apian Way.... they saw Him as He suffered and hung on the cross, but they would not see Him as the Son of God until He returns again. The Scribes and Pharisees, the Levites and the Sadducees and the corporate body of all Jews had all been blinded in part (Romans 11:25) so that they could see earthly things, but they could not see spiritual things. All turned against Jesus as a threat to their fabricated and self-centered system of worship. For centuries, they had waited for their long-awaited Messiah and here He was.... right in front of their eyes. But they refused to see and believe.

Zachariah wrote of how Israel will one day be restored as God's chosen people when Jesus returns a 2nd time.

[9] *And it shall come to pass in that day, that I will seek to destroy **all the nations that come against Jerusalem.***
[10] *And I will pour upon the house of David, and upon the inhabitants of Jerusalem, the spirit of grace and of supplications: and they shall look upon me whom they have pierced, and they shall mourn for him, as one mourns for his only son, and shall be in bitterness for him, as one that is in bitterness for his firstborn.*   Zachariah 12: 9-10

There is no doubt that Zachariah is prophesying of the Battle of Armageddon (Revelation 19).

When Titus and his Roman army destroyed Herod's Temple in 70 AD, God did not intervene. When the Muslims took over the Temple Mount and built the Dome of the Rock, He did not intervene ……but when His Son Jesus Christ returns a 2nd time, He will destroy all heathens (nations) and unbelievers that dare to come against Him. At that time, *all Israel* (those alive) *will be saved* (Romans 11: 25-26).

Hindsight being better than foresight, we now know that 40 years after the crucifixion of Jesus Christ….in 70 AD…. Titus and his Roman Centurions destroyed Herod's Temple. It was not partial but total destruction. The Temple was razed and burned and all of its inhabitants were slain. The Temple was ransacked, dismantled and completely destroyed..… not one stone was left in place. The City of Jerusalem was leveled to the ground and all but the very young and old were deported.

Although Christ barely mentioned the destruction of the Temple 40 years later in 70 AD, it is clear from the complete council of Holy Scripture and historical records that this was not the end of the Jews. They were dispersed among the nations but the chosen people of God were not destroyed. The persecution of the Jews did not end in 70 AD. The oppression during the dark ages, the annialation of over 6 million Jews by Hitler's 3rd Reich, and current antisemitism have not destroyed their race. They are God's chosen people and there are promises of God yet to be fulfilled……the Jews will never cease to exist. The Jews will be persecuted and the City of Jerusalem will always be under political, military and religious siege: *Jerusalem will be trodden down of the Gentiles until the times of the Gentiles be fulfilled* (Luke 2:24). Desecration of the Holy City Jerusalem and the Holy People the Jews will continue until they finally accept Jesus Christ as their redeemer, Lord and Savior. *When will all of this end?*

As the Church Age comes to an end, the dispersion of all Jews, the return to Israel by all 12 tribes, and the blindness of corporate Israel will end. The current return of many Jews to Israel and humanitarian efforts to provide transportation are all premature. Many prophecy teachers declare that this a sign of the end…. but this is not true (Isaiah 11: 11-12).

There have been bible scholars who maintain and teach that the destruction of Herod's Temple and the City of Jerusalem in 70 AD was taught by Jesus Christ in the Olivet Discourse, but this is blatantly incorrect. There are multiple prophecies which predict that Jerusalem will be destroyed in the Old Testament, but those Old Testament prophecies never speak of a Temple destruction in 70 AD. Zachariah clearly spoke of a future invasion of Jerusalem.

[1] *Behold, the **Day of the LORD** cometh, and thy spoil shall be divided in the midst of thee.*
[2] *For I will gather all nations against Jerusalem to battle; and the city shall be taken, and the houses rifled, and the women ravished; and half of the city shall go forth into captivity, and the residue of the people shall not be cut off from the city*   Zachariah 14: 1-2

The *Day of the Lord* is the future Battle of Armageddon (Phillips, *The Day of the Lord*). Note that on this day Satan will gather his followers from *all nations* and they will come against Jerusalem. In 70 AD, only Rome came against Jerusalem and the Temple. The Temple was completely burned and destroyed and it was replaced by the Muslim Dome of the Rock in 685 AD. The Jewish Temple will be rebuilt before the Great Tribulation begins (Matthew 24:15, II Thessalonians 2:4, Revelation 11: 1-2). We will have more to say about this later.

Note that all biblical scholars agree that the Book of Revelation was written in 90 AD or later, and Revelation 11: 1-2 cannot be referring to the destruction in 70 AD.

Not much was revealed in the Olivet Discourse about how and when Herod's Temple would be destroyed. We know now that God in His mercy gave Israel and the Jews 40 years to repent, but they would not. The Priesthood had become corrupted; both the Sadducees and the Pharisees were glad that Jesus Christ had been crucified; and the rage of the people was placated when they demanded that Jesus Christ take the place of a heinous murderer named Barabas on the Cross of Calvary.

The great Jewish historian Josephus wrote of the carnage and destruction of the Temple in 70 AD. He has often been criticized as incorrect and / or inaccurate, but he was there as an officer in the Roman army of Titus and there is no reason to doubt his eye-witness account.

The Siege of Jerusalem in 70 AD
In the spring of AD 70, Titus gathered his forces around Jerusalem. His army consisted of about 60,000 Roman legionaries, assault machines, and troops provided by regional allies. The Roman forces were well-equipped and experienced, having been engaged in both the Jewish Revolt and Roman conquests for several years. Inside the city, the Jewish defenders were in a state of disarray due to infighting among different factions. Despite this, they had prepared for the siege by storing food and fortifying the temple gates and walls.

The siege lasted approximately five months. Initially, the Romans attempted to breach the temple walls using siege towers and battering rams. When this failed, they resorted to a blockade, aiming to starve the people into submission. The conditions within the temple quickly became desperate. Food and water supply dwindled, and disease spread among those trapped inside. Fighting among the Jews who were trapped inside intensified, and the temple's defense weakened. In the summer of AD 70, the Romans finally managed to breach the Third Wall, then the Second. Finally, they penetrated the heavily fortified First Wall, entering into the Upper City.

One of the most significant and heart-wrenching events during the fall of Jerusalem was the destruction of the Second Temple. According to historical accounts, the Roman soldiers set the Temple on fire, disregarding Titus's orders to spare it. The Temple, a magnificent structure considered the heart of Jewish religious life, was reduced to ashes. The fall of Jerusalem was also accompanied by significant loss of life. Josephus provides an account of the carnage, stating that the Romans killed all of the Temple's defenders, and many of the city's inhabitants. The exact numbers are disputed and likely exaggerated in Josephus' account, but it is clear that the scale of the massacre was substantial. Those who were not killed were taken as slaves, with many sent to the mines of Egypt or sold in slave markets. The city of Jerusalem was thoroughly ransacked by the Romans. Buildings, homes, and walls were torn down, leaving the city in ruins.

The level of devastation was such that Josephus claimed that those who visited the city after its destruction could scarcely believe it had ever been inhabited. The Romans also carried off the treasures of the Temple as spoils of war, including the *Menorah*, which was famously depicted on the Arch of Titus in Rome. The final destruction of the Temple occurred on the 9th day of the Hebrew month of Av, a date that is still observed by Jews today. It is more than interesting that the 1st and 2nd Temples were both destroyed upon the exact same day.

The Arch of Titus in Rome

The disciples were still confused concerning the total devastation and destruction of the temple. Christ would speak no more of when or how the Temple would be destroyed. This would come soon enough in 70 AD. They now press Him for an answer as to *what shall be the sign of thy coming, and of the end of the world?* (Matthew 24:3). He now turns His attention to the circumstances and signs of His 2nd coming, which would be now almost 2000 years from that night.

His answer begins in Matthew 24:4. He will answer this question without any reference to the destruction of Herod's Temple because He knew that this would have nothing to do with His second coming. The prophecy which He gives is known as the *Olivet Discourse*.

Chapter 3
When Shall These Things Be?

It is difficult to understand exactly what Christ was revealing to His apostles without understanding how His words were eventually recorded in the Holy Scriptures. Greek was the language spoken by most officials of the Roman Empire. Christ spoke Hebrew, Aramaic and Greek and the Olivet Discourse was probably delivered in Hebrew or Aramaic. The words of Jesus Christ were first translated into Latin by Jerome (The Latin Vulgate), and later into Greek (Septuagint) and then into English. Contrary to popular belief, the King James Version of the Bible in 1611 AD was not the first English language version of the Bible, but built upon extensive translation activity in the 1500s. This began with the work of William Tyndale and the printing of the first English New Testament in 1526.

The Greek language is much more descriptive than the English language into which it was eventually translated. For example, a Western American might say: *this is hot*. What does this mean? In the Greek there would be no problem understanding exactly what is meant by "hot". There are 5 Greek words which could be used for "hot".

ζεστός	θερμός	καυτός
hot, warm, cosy	hot, thermal, warm, heated, fervent.	hot, boiling hot
καυτερός	καυστικός	
hot, burning	caustic, torrid, vitriolic, sweltering, poignant, hot	

The average prophecy teacher will casually use phrases like *Tribulation* and *Wrath*, but how would Christ use these words? We must understand exactly what Jesus Christ was saying when He used words like *wrath* and *tribulation*.

In the Greek language:

> ***Tulipsis*** means *Tribulation*, persecution, trouble

> ***Thumas*** means *wrath*: Uncontrolled, Fierce, Intense anger

Clearly, there is a great difference in *Tribulation* and *wrath*. As we study the words which Jesus Christ spoke in the Olivet discourse, we will sometimes use the original Greek Septuagint to help interpret His meaning. Before examining each verse of Matthew 24-25 in context, it is appropriate to note the following. When Christ spoke of *tribulation* in the Olivet Discourse, He did not mean *wrath*. He carefully divided the end-times, *Great Tribulation*, into three different time periods.

When Christ gave His *Olivet Discourse*, the Church Age had not yet begun and the Book of Revelation had not yet been written. Today, we have the advantage of the Book of Revelation and the 13 Epistles of Paul, which reveal some of the details behind the Olivet Discourse. The things written in the Book of Revelation and the prophecies written by Paul *must* coincide with the things revealed by Christ in the Olivet Discourse. As Matthew 24-25 is studied verse by verse, some but not all of the details in the Book of Revelation and the writings of Paul will be matched to the words of Christ. For a more complete exposition, see Phillips; *The Book of Revelation: Mysteries Revealed* and Phillips; *A New Pre-Wrath Rapture Theory*.

> *And as he sat upon the mount of Olives, the disciples came unto him privately, saying: Tell us, when shall these things be? and what shall be the sign of thy coming, and of the end of the world?*   Matthew 24:3

The disciples were hoping that Christ would reveal to them when He would return and establish His Kingdom. Remember that at that time, Jesus is speaking only to the Jews, and the apostles were only concerned about when Christ would return to reign with each of them (Matthew 19:28). They also knew that Christ would sit upon the throne of David to rule and reign (Luke 1: 32-33). God had also promised Abraham, Moses and King David that 12 tribes of Israel would someday inherit all of the Land of Canaan which they never conquered under Joshua (Psalms 105: 7-11). The sign which the apostles were seeking was not a sign which would herald the rapture of the church. The rapture and the catching away of all New Covenant saints was completely hidden at this time. The *sign* referred to the return of Christ to rule and reign, and to fulfill all of the covenant promises that God made to Israel. We will see later that since a remnant of Jews would accept Christ as their Lord and Savior by faith before He returns, that He *did* include veiled references to the rapture of the saints. They fully expected that He would fulfill all end-time prophecy in the near future, but Jesus did not reveal when that would take place. In fact, He actually did not know.

> *But of that day and hour knoweth no man, no, not the angels of heaven, but my Father only*   Matthew 24:36

Jesus Christ now describes the conditions which would precede His 2nd Advent.

> *[4] And Jesus answered and said unto them, Take heed that no man deceive you.*
> *[5] For many shall come in my name, saying, I am Christ; and shall*

> deceive many.
> [6] And ye shall hear of wars and rumors of wars: see that ye be not troubled: for all these things must come to pass, but the end is not yet.
> [7] For nation shall rise against nation, and kingdom against kingdom: and there shall be famines, and pestilences, and earthquakes, in divers places.
> [8] All these are the beginning of sorrows.   Matthew 24: 4-8

These words of Jesus in Matthew 24: 4-8 have been debated almost 2000 years since the Book of Revelation was written sometime between 90 AD and 96 AD by the apostle John, and the following revelation was written by John.

[1] And I saw when the Lamb opened one of the Seals, and I heard, as it were the noise of thunder, one of the four beasts saying, Come and see.
[2] And I saw, and behold a white horse: and he that sat on him had a bow; and a crown was given unto him: and he went forth conquering, and to conquer.
[3] And when he had opened the second Seal, I heard the second beast say, Come and see.
[4] And there went out another horse that was red: and power was given to him that sat thereon to take peace from the earth, and that they should kill one another: and there was given unto him a great sword.
[5] And when he had opened the third Seal, I heard the third beast say, Come and see. And I beheld, and lo a black horse; and he that sat on him had a pair of balances in his hand.
[6] And I heard a voice in the midst of the four beasts say, A measure of wheat for a penny, and three measures of barley for a penny; and see thou hurt not the oil and the wine.
[7] And when he had opened the fourth Seal, I heard the voice of the fourth beast say, Come and see.
[8] And I looked, and behold a pale horse: and his name that sat on him was Death, and Hell followed with him. And power was given unto them

over the fourth part of the earth, to kill with sword, and with hunger, and with death, and with the beasts of the earth. Revelation 6: 1-8

The agents of this devastation and persecution have been named *The 4 Horsemen of the Apocalypse*. They are described in the Book of Revelation and correspond to Seals 1-4: They bring Conquest, Famine, War, and Death.

Four Horsemen of the Apocalypse, an 1887 painting by Viktor Vasnetsov. From left to right are Death, Famine, War, and Conquest;

The controversy which exists between the words of Jesus Christ in Matthew 24: 4-8 and what John wrote in Revelation 6: 1-8 concerns the scope of death, famine, war and conquest. Many scholars insist that the impact of opening Seals 1-4 go all the way back to the prophecies of Christ in 30 AD. Others suggest that the Matthew 24: 4-8 refer to the destruction of Jerusalem and Herod's Temple in 70 AD. There should really be no controversy at all.

Keep in mind that Christ is specifically addressing His apostle's inquiry concerning signs of His 2nd coming. Hence, His warnings and observations concerning His 2nd advent *must* be identical with Revelation 6: 1-8. There have been wars, conquest, death and famine across portions of the entire planet of earth since 30 AD, but they will intensify greatly and have more impact in the Great Tribulation. There is no controversy or conflict.

Christ began by first warning that Satan would continue to lie and deceive all Jews (and Christians) until He returns (Matthew 24: 4-5). There would be many who would arise and say that *I am Christ* before the end comes. The list is large beginning with Rhys Evans in the 17th Century; and more recently Charles Mansen, Jim Jones and A. J. Miller

(wikipedia.org/wiki/List_of_people_claimed_to_be_Jesus). The severe tribulation caused by Satan will begin after he is cast down to earth (Revelation 12). He will energize an *unholy trinity* composed of Satan-Antichrist- False prophet and deceive the world. the Antichrist will arise and force all people to worship Him as the Jewish Messiah (II Thessalonians 2:4). In addition to a long list of Jesus impersonators ending with the Antichrist, there will be *Wars and rumors of Wars.* Many people believed that Hitler was the Antichrist and that the 3rd Reich would rule over Europe as a 10-Nation confederacy, but they were wrong. The Great Tribulation cannot begin until Satan is cast out of the heavenlies and the 7 Trumpets begin to sound.

There will be an increasing unrest and conflict worldwide as the period of Great Tribulation described in the Book of Revelation nears. There will be *wars and rumors of wars* and a great falling away of Christians and faith (II Peter 2, Jude 1): There will be an increase in *famines* and *earthquakes*: but be not alarmed or lose faith. Wars and global conflicts are *not* signs that Christ will return at any minute, but a prophesied state of rebellion and unrest around the whole world. The conflicts, wars, famines and earthquakes which will become more frequent are just another sign that the period of Tribulation and Wrath is not far away. As the Great Tribulation nears, there can never be world peace because man is decidedly wicked and *many will turn from the faith*. The destruction of Jerusalem and the Temple of Herod in 70 AD and the Jewish Holocaust are only the *beginning of sorrows*.

All these are the beginning of sorrows	Matthew 24:8

> ***Authors Comment***: This author will suggest that there will be a visible *sign* which will be seen by all that will launch the *Great Tribulation*. That *sign* will be a great heavenly conflict between Micheal and his Holy Angels and Satan and his Unholy Angels (Revelation 12:7). I believe that this conflict will be seen by

everyone, and that communication and television has reached the point where it will be televised. This will immediately precede the last 3.5 years of this age, and the sign of a great war in heaven cannot be ignored or missed. When Satan is cast down, he will be full of great *Thumas* or uncontrollable rage (Revelation 12:12). A great European political and military leader will be the dictator of a 10-Nation European coalition (Daniel 7: 23-25). He will be killed with a knife or sword (Revelation 13: 1-3, Revelation 13:14, Daniel 7:11). Satan will then use his earthly body to become what we call the *Antichrist* to make war on mankind (Daniel 7:25, Revelation 23:7). He will end a peace treaty with Israel which will be called the *Covenant of Death* (Isaiah 28: 15-18), attack Jerusalem and invade the new Temple. He will then sit in the Holy Place and declare Himself to be worshipped as God (II Thessalonians 2:4). This was predicted by Christ (Matthew 24: 15-16). Paul later verified the words of Christ in his letter to the church at Thessalonica.

[1] *Now we beseech you, brethren, by the coming of our Lord Jesus Christ, and by our gathering together unto him,*
[2] *That ye be not soon shaken in mind, or be troubled, neither by spirit, nor by word, nor by letter as from us, as that the day of Christ is at hand.*
[3] *Let no man deceive you by any means: for that day shall not come, except there comes a falling away first, and that man of sin be revealed, the son of perdition;*
[4] *Who opposes and exalts himself above all that is called God, or that is worshipped; so that he as God sits in the temple of God, shewing himself that he is God.*
[5] *Remember ye not, that, when I was yet with you, I told you these things?*   II Thessalonians 2 1-5

> Satan as the Antichrist will force those who capitulate to take the *mark of the beast*. Failure to do so will result in spiritual death (Revelation 13:15). Those who refuse to take the Mark of the Beast will be easily recognized: No one can buy or sell without this mark (Revelation 13:17). BEWARE…Those who take this mark will condemn themselves forever to the Lake of Burning Fire…BEWARE (Revelation 20:15).

The first 4 signs that Jesus gave to recognize His 2nd Advent have been the subject of debate for many years. In Revelation 5: 1-14, John sees God the Father standing before His throne and He is holding a 6-Sealed Scroll in His right hand. John has previously been given an outline of what he has been told to write.

*Write **the things which thou hast seen**, and **the things which are**, and **the things which shall be hereafter***   Revelation 1:19

These instructions which Christ gave to John on the Island of Patmos divide the Book of Revelation into three different periods of time. The ***things which thou hast seen*** (Revelation 1: 1-20): The ***things which are*** (Revelation 2:1 - Revelation 5:14) and ***the things which shall be hereafter*** (Revelation 6:1 - Revelation 22:20). It is extremely important to put everything in the Book of Revelation into proper context. Everything from Matthew 24:9 - Matthew 25:46, and Revelation 6:1 – Revelation 22:20 is future to when they Book Revelation was written in the 1st century AD. Matthew 24: 1-7 and Revelation 6: 1-8 have caused a great deal of confusion between the Olivet Discourse and future end-time events. Christ spoke the Olivet Discourse in 30 AD, and He prophesied that there would be death, famine, wars and conquests before He would return.

The effect of opening Seals 1-4 in the Book of Revelation should specifically be applied to the *Great Tribulation*. Everything from Revelation 5:1 to Revelation 22:20 is in the future.

The 1st four Seals described in Revelation 6: 1-8 predict that the *Great Tribulation* will bring unprecedented persecution and suffering upon both Jews and Christians. The conditions which are predicted in Revelation 6: 1-8 are not time-delay events but describe general conditions which will exist during the Great Tribulation, just as the same conditions described in Matthew 24: 1-7 span the Church Age. They are not one-time events. It is necessary to show that the 7 Seals which are broken and removed by Jesus Christ ***cannot*** be time-sequenced events in lock-step with the 7 Trumpet Judgments and the 7 Bowl Judgments.

The 7 Seals: Traditional Chronology

An overwhelming majority of biblical scholars teach that the 7 Seals, the 7 Trumpets and the 7 Bowls are executed *sequentially* over a 7-year period of time. The duration of each set will depend upon which article

Figure 1

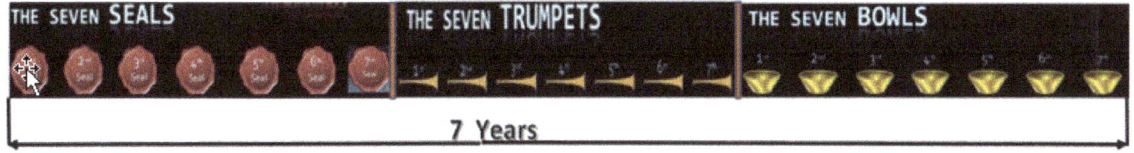

Figure 2

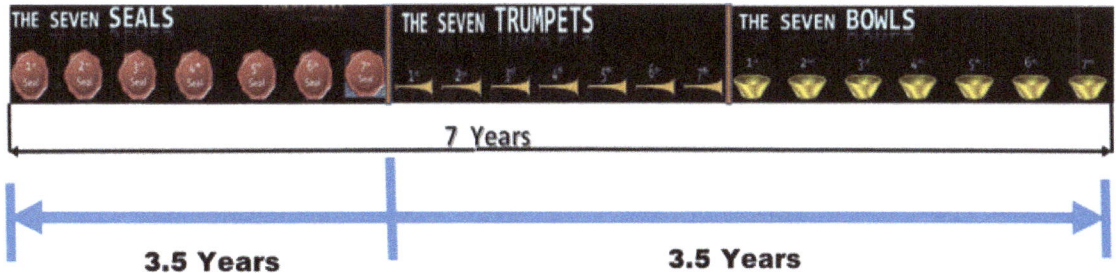

Figure 3

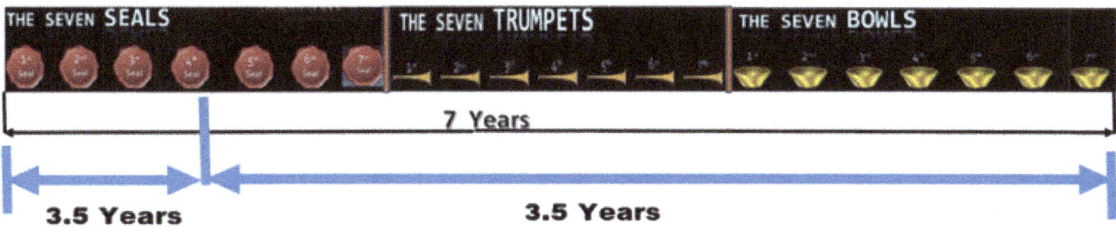

or book one reads. The following three scenarios are typical. The 1st three Seals are almost always placed during the first 3.5 years of the Tribulation period. The 1st three Seals represent conditions that one might expect when war and conflict might break out (No peace, inflation & hunger).

The 4th Seal is more specific. The result of the 4th Seal is that ¼ of all people upon the earth will perish.

Seal 5 is a prophetic interlude concerning those who will be martyred for Christ. They are seen beneath the throne of God (Revelation 6: 9-10), and they cry out for vengeance. God gives each one a white robe and tells them to wait awhile… more of their brothers must be killed.

Authors Comment: It is not clear whether these martyrs that are seen beneath the throne of God are from all ages past, or just those who will be killed for Jesus Christ during the Great tribulation. Since we will now show that as Seals 1-6 are removed by Christ, each predict either general conditions (Seals 1-5) which will characterize the Great Tribulation, or several specific events which are described when Seal 6 is broken, it is likely that those saints who have been martyred and are seen beneath the throne come from the Great Tribulation. They have paid the ultimate price for their faith in Jesus Christ and are immediately taken beneath the Throne of God when they are Martyred.

[12] And I beheld when he had opened the sixth Seal, and, lo, there was a great earthquake; and the sun became black as sackcloth of hair, and the moon became as blood;
[13] And the stars of heaven fell unto the earth, even as a fig tree casts her untimely figs, when she is shaken of a mighty wind.
[14] And the heavens departed as a scroll when it is rolled together; and every mountain and island were moved out of their places.
[15] And the kings of the earth, and the great men, and the rich men, and the chief captains, and the mighty men, and every bondman, and every free man, hid themselves in the dens and in the rocks of the mountains;
[16] And said to the mountains and rock: Fall on us, and hide us from the face of him that sits on the throne, and from the wrath of the Lamb:
[17] For the great day of his wrath is come; and who shall be able to stand?   Revelation 6: 12-17

When the 6th Seal is removed: (1) There is a great earthquake (2) The sun turns black and the moon turns red (3) The heavens depart as when a scroll is rolled up (4) *Every mountain and every island are moved out of their place* (5) The Kings of the earth hide in rocks and caves because: (6) The *Wrath of God* has come.

When the 7th Seal is removed, there is complete silence in heaven for about half an hour. Clearly, something is about to happen that stuns all of the creatures and angels which surround the Throne of God. They all fall silent because the scroll can now be unrolled and the 7 Trumpets and 7 Bowls can be described. Read these verses (Revelation 6: 12-17) very carefully…. Study them and memorize what will happen as the 6th Seal is removed. The following analysis will challenge

25

all you may have been told about the sequential nature of the 7 Seals, the 7 Trumpets and the 7 Bowls.

The vast majority of all prophecy teachers, pastors and scholars will resolutely declare that: The 7 Seals, 7 Trumpets and 7 Bowl Judgments are serial in nature, and once the 1st Seal is removed 21 events will occur in sequence (See Figures 1-3). We will now show that this is an incorrect and untenable theology.

The 7 Seals: Correct Chronology
The 7 Seals must all be removed before the contents of the 7-Seal scroll can be revealed to the Apostle John. The 7 Seals are broken and removed by Jesus Christ (Revelation 5:5). The scroll contains a description of what will occur as the Church Age draws to a close. As each of the 6 Seals are removed, John is shown *visions* of the future which would later be fulfilled. Seals 1-5 only predict *conditions* and (Seal 6) predicts several *specific* events which will later take place during the Great Tribulation. Seal 7 is a 30-minute period of heavenly silence.

THE SEALED SCROLL

Note that each of the 7 Trumpets and the 7 Bowls are delivered to the earth from heaven by mighty angels at the command of God (Revelation 8:2, Revelation 15:1), but only Christ removes the 7-Seals. Even though there is a direct relationship between the Seals, Trumpets and Bowls … there is a distinct difference between them. The 7 Seals only *reveal* things to come: The 7 Trumpets and the 7 Bowls actually *cause* things to happen. John was actually to *see* visions of the scrolls contents once the 7 Seals are removed (Revelation 6: 1,3,7… Etc.). This scroll contains the eternal plan of God to fulfill all of His covenant promises to the Nation of Israel. He had promised His beloved Israel that one day He would place them in the land of promise and that they would dwell there. This *unconditional* covenant promise of God will be fulfilled in the 1000-year Millennial Kingdom. The purpose of the Great Tribulation is to fully restore the Jews into an intimate and personal relationship with God as He intended all along, and to inaugurate His Son Jesus Christ as the sovereign King who will rule and reign beside King David. Only God can do this, and He will do it to exalt and honor His Son Jesus Christ.

[18] But those things, which God before had showed by the mouth of all his prophets, that Christ should suffer, he hath so fulfilled.
[19] Repent ye therefore, and be converted, that your sins may be blotted out, when the times of refreshing shall come from the presence of the Lord;
[20] And he shall send Jesus Christ, which before was preached unto you:
[21] Whom *the heaven must receive until the times of restitution of all things, which God hath spoken by the mouth of all his holy prophets since the world began* Acts 3: 18-21

[18] The eyes of your understanding being enlightened; that ye may know what is the hope of his calling, and what the riches of the glory of his inheritance in the saints,
[19] And what is the exceeding greatness of his power to usward who believe, according to the working of his mighty power,
[20] Which he wrought in Christ, when he raised him from the dead, and set him at his own right hand in the heavenly places,
[21] Far above all principality, and power, and might, and dominion, and every name that is named, not only in this world, but also in that which is to come:
[22] And hath put all things under his feet, and gave him to be the head over all things to the church,
[23] Which is his body, the fulness of him that fills all in all
Ephesians 1: 18-23

As Christ begins to remove the 7 Seals, John is shown what will take place as this *Church Age* comes to an end. The first vision comes as the 1st Seal is removed.

[1] And I saw when the Lamb opened one of the Seals, and I heard, as it were the noise of thunder, one of the four beasts saying, Come and see. [2] And I saw, and behold a white horse: and he that sat on him had a bow; and a crown was given unto him: and he went forth conquering, and to conquer   Revelation 6: 1-2

As Christ breaks the 1st Seal, one of the 4 beasts that stand before the throne of God tells John: *Come and see* (Revelation 6:1). As John obeys, he sees a white horse and a rider which has a bow but no arrows. The rider comes forth to conquer (Revelation 6:2). This rider has long been debated. Many have identified the rider of this horse as Jesus Christ, but this is entirely out of context with Seals 2-4. This rider has a bow but no arrows: He will conquer with military power as well as political cunning. It is not Jesus Christ who rides forth on a white horse. It is not exclusively Satan, and in context with the other three riders it cannot be the Antichrist. The horses and riders are purely symbolic. All 4 horses and riders personify and represent both supernatural and devastating forces that will be at work during the Great Tribulation. After careful consideration, it is suggested and concluded that the 1st rider represents the deception, cunning and political power of Satan during the Great Tribulation (He has a bow but no arrows).

**First Seal
Rider on White Horse**

Rider has a bow
Rider wears a crown
Rider goes forth Conquering

Revelation 6: 1-2

> For there shall arise false Christs, and false prophets, and shall shew great signs and wonders; insomuch that, if it were possible, they shall deceive the very elect   Matthew 24:24

The Antichrist and False Prophet will fulfil these words of Christ. They will deceive many, and condemn those who reject Christ as their Lord and Savior to everlasting judgment in the Lake of Fire. This will be manifested throughout the duration of the Great Tribulation and will be accompanied by what each of the first 4 Seals predict: *Destruction, Wars, Famine,* and *Death*.

As the second Seal is broken/removed, John is again commanded to *come and see,* and he sees a rider on a Red Horse.

[3] *And when he had opened the second Seal, I heard the second beast say, Come and see.*
[4] *And there went out another horse that was red: and power was given to him that sat thereon to take peace from the earth, and that they should kill one another: and there was given unto him a great sword*
Revelation 6: 3-4

This rider is given a *great sword*. This sword represents the instrument by which peace will be removed from all of the earth. Men will war against one another and kill one another. *Is this horse and great sword the only instrument of war?* Likely not. In the 1st century there were no helicopters, tanks or airplanes and John is conveying the instruments of war which will be used over 2000 years later as best he can. It is better to interpret the sword which takes peace from the world as a symbol of destruction and death over an extended period of time…. characterized by conflict, terror and bloodshed. Satan will conquer by using supernatural powers granted by God and the military power of the final 10-Nation confederacy (Daniel 7, Revelation 13). The 2nd rider represents the power to make war. His instrument of power and destruction will be the Antichrist (Revelation 13: 1-10). The 3rd Seal is now removed by Christ.

[5] And when he had opened the third Seal, I heard the third beast say, Come and see. And I beheld, and lo a black horse; and he that sat on him had a pair of balances in his hand.
[6] And I heard a voice in the midst of the four beasts say, A measure of wheat for a penny, and three measures of barley for a penny; and see thou hurt not the oil and the wine   Revelation 6: 5-6

When Jesus Christ opens the 3rd Seal. John is told to *come and see.* A black horse appears with a rider which has a scale in his right hand. This scale is one which was commonly used to weigh grain. A counterweight was used to determine the purchase price. The rider clothed in black and the scales indicate that a time is coming of sorrow and suffering due to a shortage and scarcity of food. *What could cause such a worldwide lack of food?*

This is a prediction of what will occur when Trump 1 and Trump 2 sounds (Revelation 8: 7-9), and will be completed when the 7 Bowl Judgments are unleashed upon the earth (Revelation 16: 1-21). When Trump 1 sounds *all* green grass is burned up along with 1/3 of all the trees (Revelation 8:7). If something burns up *all* the green grass, crops and trees will largely be burned up also. There will not only be devastating fires, but when the 3rd Trumpet sounds, 1/3 of all the fresh water will be polluted in some supernatural way (Revelation 8:10). The devastation of crops and food when Trump 1 and Trump 2 are blown is bad enough, but when the 3rd Bowl is poured out, *all* fresh water (rivers, streams and water wells) turn to blood. The 3rd Bowl in the sequence of seven will affect all the earth very near the end of the Tribulation period. Man can be denied food for an extended period of time, but water is necessary to sustain life. Medical research has determined that the average person can live only 3-4 days without water. When all bottled water and liquids are consumed, mankind would only survive days. The 4th Seal is now removed.

[7] *And when he had opened the fourth Seal, I heard the voice of the fourth beast say, Come and see.*
[8] *And I looked, and behold a pale horse: and his name that sat on him was Death, and Hell followed with him. And power was given unto them over the fourth part of the earth, to kill with sword, and with hunger, and with death, and with the beasts of the earth*   Revelation 6: 7-8

As the 4th Seal is broken, John turns to see a pale horse. In Greek, the phrase translated as pale horse (KJV) means a sickly, yellowish-green color. The rider of this horse is *death*. The 1st Seal has brought deception by force or cunning. The 2nd Seal brings war....and war always brings famine and devastation. The 3rd Seal predicts severe *worldwide* poverty and famine. The 4th Seal reveals a pale horse, and it its rider is *death*. ¼ of all the world's population will die. War and famine always result in death. This is a serious warning of what is about to take place as the Great Tribulation begins is about to start. The agents of destruction described by Seals 1-4 have been portrayed by most biblical scholars as The *Four Horsemen of the Apocalypse*. The role of the 7-Seals (Revelation 6: 1-8) has been almost totally misunderstood by modern

prophecy teachers. The description of the first 6 Seals in the Book of Revelation occurs immediately after Chapter 5: 1-4, which describes how the Scroll with 7 Seals is seen in God's right hand. This scroll contains a description of how the Church Age will end in a period of Great Tribulation; what the Millennial Kingdom will bring; and how the earth will be purged of all sin and renovated by God after the 1000-year Millennial Kingdom. Matthew 24: 1-12 and Revelation 6: 1-8 are both describing exactly the same thing, but the scope is different. When Jesus Christ spoke the Olivet Discourse, he was describing conditions which would take place over the next 2000 years, and specifically as Titus and his Roman Centurions destroyed the City and the Temple. Jesus Christ predicted these same conditions would occur over the Great Tribulation, more severely than ever before.

> For then shall be great tribulation, such as was not since the beginning of the world to this time, no, nor ever shall be   Matthew 24:21

The reality is that over the past 2000 years Satan has always caused deception, wars, famine and pestilence throughout the world. The destruction of Herod's Temple in 70 AD was not the fulfillment of the Olivet Discourse, but it was just the beginning of these trials and tribulations. One could easily argue that the persecution of Jews during WW II and the 3rd Reich was unprecedented in all previous years of history. It is estimated that over 6 million Jews were slaughtered and killed, and another 2 million fled into hiding during the holocaust. The Jews have never fully recovered from the impact of WW II and the Jewish Holocaust, but according to the words of Jesus Christ, things will get worse when the *Wrath of Satan* is unleashed during the 7 Trumpet Judgments and the *Wrath of God* falls upon all unbelievers (Revelation 15:1, Revelation 15:7, Revelation 16:1).

The *Great Tribulation* will begin when Satan is cast out of heaven (Revelation 12: 7-8) and he will be furious with rage (Revelation 12:17). He will totally dominate and inherit the body of a slain European world leader and arise as the *Antichrist* (Revelation 13: 3-16). He will break a peace treaty with Israel which has allowed them to build a new temple in Jerusalem.

*Because ye have said: We have made a **Covenant with Death**, and with hell are we at agreement; when the overflowing scourge shall pass through, it shall not come unto us: for we have made lies our refuge, and under falsehood have we hid ourselves   Isaiah 28:15*

Israel will be deceived and think that they are living in peace and safety. Suddenly, Satan as the Antichrist will turn upon Israel and annul the *Covenant of Peace* which was in reality a *Covenant of Death*.

*And your **Covenant with Death** shall be disannulled, and your agreement with hell shall not stand; when the overflowing scourge shall pass through, then ye shall be trodden down by it*   Zachariah 28:18

As soon as Satan is cast out of heaven, Satan will attack Jerusalem in what we have called the *Jerusalem Campaign* (Phillips, The Book of Revelation: *Mysteries Revealed*). He will pursue a fleeing remnant of Jews into the wilderness (Revelation 12: 14-15). Just as all hope seems to be lost, God will miraculously save these people with what appears to be a great earthquake (Revelation 12: 14-15). Satan as the Antichrist will be furious (Revelation 12:17a). He will then turn on all Jews and Christians (Revelation 12: 17b). During his 3.5 years reign of terror, he will kill 2/3 of all Jews (Zachariah 13: 8-9). In Zachariah Chapter 14: 1-16, the Prophet describes things which will happen at the *Battle of Armageddon….* which will take place at the Second Advent of Christ. If one will carefully read Zachariah 14, there can be no doubt that when Christ returns to fight the Battle of Armageddon this is the *Day of the Lord*. It is also true that the Day of the Lord is exactly what we have said it is… *one day* (Phillips, *The Day of the Lord*).

*But it shall be **one day** which shall be known to the LORD, not day, nor night: but it shall come to pass, that at evening time it shall be light* Zachariah 14:7

Be sure about it......the 4th Seal did not cause these things to happen ......they will take place as the 7 Trumpets and the 7 Bowls take place over the last 3.5 years of the Church Age. The 5th Seal is now broken.

[9] And when he had opened the fifth Seal, I saw under the altar the souls of them that were slain for the word of God, and for the testimony which they held:
[10] And they cried with a loud voice, saying, How long, O Lord, holy and true, dost thou not judge and avenge our blood on them that dwell on the earth?
[11] And white robes were given unto every one of them; and it was said unto them, that they should rest yet for a little season, until their fellow-servants also and their brethren, that should be killed as they were, should be fulfilled   Revelation 6: 9-11

As the 5th Seal is broken, John is shown a remarkable vision concerning the Christians who have been martryed rather than deny Jesus Christ. The death and destruction predicted as the first four Seals are broken will prove to be the ultimate test of faith to many Christians who will not bow down to the Antichrist. Many will not publicly deny their faith in Christ and be put to death (Revelation 13: 14-15). Once again, it should be clear that the opening of the 5th Seal is not an *event* that will happen all at once, but something that will happen *throughout the duration* of the last 3.5 years of this age. This is a remarkable prophecy.... the souls of all faithful martyrs are seen *beneath the throne of God* (Revelation 6: 9-11). Their suffering and faith to the death is evidently so great that when they are martyred for Christ they are immediately taken to a place beneath the heavenly throne of God. They cry out for vengeance:

And they cried with a loud voice, saying, how long, O Lord, holy and true, dost thou not judge and avenge our blood on them that dwell on the earth?   Revelation 6:10

The response to this plea is both revealing and immediate.

And white robes were given unto every one of them; and it was said unto them, that they should rest yet for a little season, until their fellow servants also and their brethren, that should be killed as they were, should be fulfilled   Revelation 6:11

This scene has been captured by the words of Robert L. Thomas.

> These words were spoken by Jesus Christ to the souls under God's throne. This gave them complete assurance that He will avenge their blood, but the time has not yet arrived for the culmination of that vengeance. There must still be others who will be tested, tried and martyred for Christ. Death will take an even greater toll on those on the earth just before Christ returns. Until then, those who have already been martyred can rest in the assurance that they will be avenged and attain eternal life.

A question which must be asked is: *From what dispensation of time did these martyrs come from?* Revelation 6:9 tells us that: *I saw under the altar the souls of them that were slain for the word of God, and for the testimony which they held*. This seems to indicate that these martyrs come from when Adam fell to the 2nd advent of Christ. Apostles, disciples of Christ, and New Testament evangelists for Jesus Christ have been slain through recorded time. This holy and blameless group of martyrs will not be complete until the 3.5 years of Satans reign of terror have come to an end. It appears that they will be raised in a special resurrection just before the 1000 Millennial kingdom begins.

...and I saw the souls of them that were beheaded for the witness of Jesus, and for the word of God, and which had not worshipped the beast, neither his image, neither had received his mark upon their foreheads, or in their hands; and they lived and reigned with Christ a thousand years.   Revelation 20:4b

We have shown mounting evidence that the 7 Seals are not in lock-step with the 7 Trumpets and 7 Bowls, but they only preview and overview things which will take place during the last 3.5 years of the Church Age.

The Seals consume no time and do not precede the Trumpet or Bowl Judgments in lock-step time delays as is commonly taught. When the 6th Seal is broken *possibility* becomes *certainty*.

[12] And I beheld when he had opened the sixth Seal, and, lo, there was a great earthquake; and the sun became black as sackcloth of hair, and the moon became as blood;
[13] And the stars of heaven fell unto the earth, even as a fig tree casts her untimely figs, when she is shaken of a mighty wind.
[14] And the **heaven departed as a scroll when it is rolled together; and every mountain and island were moved out of their places**
Revelation 6: 12-14

When the 6th Seal is broken, unprecedented heaven and earthly disturbances are prophesied. (1) The sun becomes black (2) The moon turns blood red (3) Stars fall from the sky (4) Heaven rolls up like a scroll. *When do these things occur in the Period of Great Tribulation?*

This question was answered by the prophet Joel.

[1] Blow ye the Trumpet in Zion, and sound an alarm in my holy mountain: let all the inhabitants of the land tremble: for the **Day of the LORD** *cometh, for it is nigh at hand;*
[2] A Day of **darkness and of gloominess**, **a day** *of clouds and of thick darkness, as the morning spread upon the mountains: a great people and a strong; there hath not been ever the like, neither shall be any more after it, even to the years of many generations*   Joel 2: 1-2

[2] I will also gather all Nations, and will bring them down into the **Valley of Jehoshaphat**, *and will plead with them there for my people*

and for my heritage Israel, whom they have scattered among the Nations, and parted my land.   Joel 3:2

[14] *Multitudes, multitudes in the* **valley of decision***: for the* **Day of the LORD** *is near in the valley of decision.*
[15] The sun and the moon shall be darkened, and the stars shall withdraw their shining.
[16] *The LORD also shall roar out of Zion, and utter his voice from Jerusalem;* **and the heavens and the earth shall shake***: but the LORD will be the hope of his people, and the strength of the children of Israel.*
Joel 3: 14-16

Joel clearly says that a **Day of the Lord** is coming and that it will be a day of darkness and gloom. A day of earthquakes, and a day in which the sun will be darkened and the stars cease to shine. There can be no doubt that this Day of the Lord is the **Battle of Armageddon** (Compare Joel 3: 14-16 to Revelation 6: 12-14). If Joel can be believed (and he can), that day will not be months and years but a *single day*. The Battle of Armageddon (Joel 3:2), will be fought following the 7 Bowl Judgments (*Wrath of God*) on the last day of the Great Tribulation. Joel continues his vision.

[30] *And I will shew wonders in the heavens and in the earth,* blood, *and fire, and pillars of smoke.*
[31] *The sun shall be turned into darkness, and the* **moon into blood***, before the great and the terrible Day of the LORD come*
Joel 2: 30-31

This should settle three key issues: This describes exactly the same events which Christ prophesied and revealed to John as He broke the 6th Seal in Revelation 6: 12-14. The evidence is complete and overwhelming: (1) The **Day of the Lord** is a **single day** on which Christ will descend from heaven and fight the *Battle of Armageddon*. (2) Removal of the 6th seal prophesies of events which should occur late in the Great Tribulation. Do not fail to recognize the significance of the next observation. (3) When the 6th Seal is removed by God; ***every island and mountain will be moved out of its place*** (Revelation 6: 14). The things shown to John as the 6th Seal is broken ***coincide*** with the pouring out of the *7th Bowl*.

[17] *And the seventh angel poured out his vial into the air; and there came a great voice out of the temple of heaven, from the throne, saying,* ***It is done****.*
[18] *And there were voices, and thunders, and lightnings; and there was **a great earthquake, such as was not since men were upon the earth**, so mighty an earthquake, and so great.*
[19] *And the great city was divided into three parts, and the cities of the Nations fell: and great Babylon came in remembrance before God, to give unto her the cup of the wine of the fierceness of **His Wrath**.*
[20] ***And every island fled away, and the mountains were not found****.*
[21] *And there fell upon men a great hail out of heaven, every stone about the weight of a talent: and men blasphemed God because of the plague of the hail; for the plague thereof was exceeding great*
Revelation 16: 17-21

It is time to Review Revelation 6:14 and Revelation 16:20 to present the most compelling and convincing evidence that the 7 Seals only review events which are about to happen as the Great Tribulation begins. As Christ removes the 6th Seal, the following description of things to come are revealed to John.

And every island fled away, and the mountains were not found.
Revelation 16:20

This exactly coincides with what will happen when the 7th Bowl is poured out upon all unbelievers.
And every island fled away, and the mountains were not found.
Revelation 16:20

This is a specific, devastating event which will occur at *only one moment in time*. *Every* mountain and island will be moved and disappear. Such an event cannot be comprehended and even imagined. Now, apply scriptural evidence and common sense to the Revelation Record. *Are we to believe that this incredible event will happen twice? ...Once when the 6th Seal is broken* (Revelation 6:14) *and again at the end of the tribulation period when the 7th Bowl is poured out* (Revelation 16:20)? Such a conclusion cannot possibly be believed or sustained!!! The *Day of the Lord* is not a protracted period of time necessitated by a Pre-Tribulation theology or a Pre-Wrath theology but *one day*. Both Pre-Tribbers and Classical Pre-Wrath Rapture supporters *must* declare that the Day of the Lord is a period of time which spans both the 7 Trumpet and the 7 Bowl Judgments because Seal 6 reveals:

For the great day of his wrath is come; and who shall be able to stand? Revelation 6:17

The conclusion .... beyond any reasonable doubt....is that when the 6th Seal is broken by Christ, John is shown what will happen just before Christ returns a 2nd time as King of Kings and Lord of Lords....not as a suffering servant but as a conquering King. The 6th Seal did not cause this to happen, it only predicted that it would.

> ***Authors Comment***: The Classic Pre-Wrath Rapture Theory was proposed by Rosenthal in a 1990 book (The Pre-Wrath Rapture of the Church in1990. This was quickly followed by Van Kampen in a1992 with a book called The Sign. Both were reading Revelation 6:17 and noticed that John wrote: the great day of his wrath is come. There are numerous scriptural references which state that Christians are not destined to go through the Wrath of God (Romans 5:9, Romans 1:18, John 3:36, Colossians 3:6, I Thessalonians 1:10, I Thessalonians 5:9). Since Revelation 6:17 reveals that *wrath is come*. They concluded that the rapture of all saints must occur as the 6th seal is removed by Christ. Note that this demands that the

Wrath of God is *both* the 7 Trumpet Judments followed by the 7 Bowl judgments and that the Day of the Lord is not a single day but a period of 3.5 years. Hence, they both made *three* fatal errors: *First*, they failed to recognize the difference between the Wrath of Satan (7 Trumpet Judgments …Revelation 12:12) and the Wrath of God (7 Bowl Judgments… Revelation 15:1, Revelation 16:1) *Second*, the effects of the 6th Seal do not precede the 7 Trumpet Judgments and the 7 Bowl Judgments, but they preview what is about to happen over the 3.5 years. *Third*, the Wrath of God is without debate the 7 Bowl Judgments (Revelation 15:1, Revelation 16:1) *Fourth*, the Day of the Lord is only *one day*, not a period of 3.5 years (Isaiah 2: 2-17, Isaiah 34:8, Jeremiah 46:10, Joel 2, Joel 3)

The universal teaching concerning the 7 Seals, the 7 Trumpets, and the 7 Bowls by all Pre-tribulation and Classic Pre-Wrath Rapturists is that the Seals, Bowls, and Trumpets are all time delay events which occur in sequence. This demands a protracted period of time of more than 3.5 years which all called the *Wrath of God* because of Revelation 6:17 which is part of the 6th Seal. This misinterpretation of prophecy is due to failure of all Pre-Tribulation advocates and Classic Pre-Wrath teachers to recognize three important truths: (1) The 7 seals are opened by Jesus Christ and must be broken and removed before the 7-Sealed Scroll can be unrolled; and the 7 Trumpet Judgments and the 7 Bowl Judgments can be described (2) There is a difference between the Wrath of Satan and the Wrath of God. The Wrath of Satan will be unleashed as the 7 Trumpets sound and the Wrath of God are the 7 Bowl/Vial Judgments … Revelation 15:1, Revelation 16:1 (3) The *Day of the Lord* is a *single day* when Jesus Christ will return to fight the Battle of Armageddon. Based upon evidence presented, the universal teaching that the Seals are in lock-step with both the 7 Trumpet Judgments and the 7 Bowl Judgments must be rejected.

Finally, note that the 6th Seal also *predicts* that a great earthquake will happen at some time in the near future, so great that such has never occurred since time began.

*And I beheld when he had opened the sixth Seal, and, lo, there was a **great earthquake**;* Revelation 6: 12a

This **great earthquake** which was predicted as the 6th Seal is removed (Revelation 6:12) will occur as the 7th and last Bowl/vial is poured out (Revelation 16:18).

[17] And the seventh angel poured out his vial into the air; and there came a great voice out of the temple of heaven, from the throne, saying: ***It is done***.
*[18] And there were voices, and thunders, and lightnings; and there was a **great earthquake**, such as was not since men were upon the earth, so mighty an earthquake, and so great* Revelation 16: 17-18

We have shown convincing evidence that when each of the 6 Seals are broken by Christ, John is shown a preview (Seals 1-4, Seal 6) of things to come (Seal 5 shows tribulation martyrs beneath the throne. Seal 7 is silence in heaven for about 30 minutes). The Great Tribulation is about to begin.

> *[9] Then shall they deliver you up to be afflicted, and shall kill you: and ye shall be hated of all Nations for my name's sake.*
> *[10] And then shall many be offended, and shall betray one another, and shall hate one another.*
> *[11] And many false prophets shall rise, and shall deceive many.*
> *[12] And because iniquity shall abound, the love of many shall wax cold.*
> *[13] But he that shall endure unto the end, the same shall be saved*
> Matthew 24: 9-13

Jews and Christians will both experience a time of persecution on a worldwide scale that will be unprecedented (Matthew 24:21). When the Antichrist breaks the *Treaty of Death* (Isaiah 28: 15,18) with Israel and sits in the temple demanding that He be worshipped as God (II Thessalonians 2:4), he will do an astounding and unbelievable thing. He will make a graven image of himself that will actually be able to think and speak (Revelation 13:15). This image will be placed in every city and town throughout the entire world: Failure to worship this image of the beast (Antichrist) will be killed (Revelation 13:15). BE WARNED! No person can buy or sell unless they have the mark of the beast upon their right hand or upon their forehead (Revelation 13:17).

*[**15**] And he had power to give life unto the image of the beast, that the image of the beast should both speak, and cause that as many as would not worship the image of the beast should be killed.*

*[**16**] And he causes all, both small and great, rich and poor, free and bond, to receive a mark in their right hand, or in their foreheads:*
*[**17**] And that no man might buy or sell, save he that had the mark, or the name of the beast, or the number of his name*
*[**18**] Here is wisdom. Let him that hath understanding count the number of the beast: for it is the number of a man; and his number is Six hundred threescore and six.*   Revelation 13: 15-18

WARNING! If anyone receives this mark on either their hand or forehead, it is an irreversible and final decision. That person is doomed to be cast into the Lake of Burning Fire (Revelation 14: 9-10).

And the beast was taken, and with him the false prophet that wrought miracles before him, with which he deceived them that had received the mark of the beast, and them that worshipped his image. These both were cast alive into a lake of fire burning with brimstone   Revelation 19:20

This will be a terrible time for all Jews and Christians upon the earth. Christ warns that:

> *And then shall many be offended, and shall betray one another, and shall hate one another*   Matthew 24:8

Timothy warned us that these things must come to pass in the end-times.

[1] *This know also, that in the last days perilous times shall come.*
[2] *For men shall be lovers of their own selves, covetous, boasters, proud, blasphemers,* **disobedient to parents**, *unthankful, unholy,*
[3] **Without natural affection**, *trucebreakers, false accusers, incontinent, fierce, despisers of those that are good,*
[4] *Traitors, heady, high-minded,* **lovers of pleasures more than lovers of God**   II Timoty 3: 1-4

It grieves my soul to see what is happening to children today. There is no discipline allowed either at home or in school. Women dress like harlots in the public, and teenagers are allowed to go to school and church with halter tops and shorts. Young adults are turning away from living a holy, righteous life to one with drugs and alcohol to erase any knowledge of holiness and righteousness. Television is saturated with same sex couples promoting *unnatural affection* (II Timothy 3:3). Society has twisted their mind into believing that they should be what they desire to be, rather than how God made them. Gender is no longer defined by one's anatomy; it is about who Satan wants them to be. There are many different gender identities, including male, female, transgender, gender neutral, non-binary, agender, pangender, genderqueer, two-spirit, third gender, none or a combination of these. If anyone wants to know whether they are male or female, just look on their birth certificate to see how God has made them. God help us but Timothy has warned us 2000 years ago that this would happen.

> *But he that shall endure unto the end, the same shall be saved*
> Matthew 24:13

What does this mean? Cults, churches founded to please man and not God, and religious sects such as the Armenians teach that salvation can only be granted to those who live a righteous life and virtuous life. These self-professed "Christians" not only deceive themselves, but insult Jesus Christ who died a horrible, sinless sacrificial death for our sins.

[8] *For by grace are ye saved through faith; and that not of yourselves: it is the gift of God:*
[9] *Not of works, lest any man should boast.*   Ephesians 2: 8-9

No one deserves to go to heaven because all have sinned and fallen short of the Glory of God. Endurance and good deeds have nothing to do with salvation by grace and faith. There is not one verse in all of the Holy Scripture that contradicts that salvation is based upon the atoning sacrifice of Jesus Christ and His work of permanently forgiving all sins when He was crucified and died on the Cross of Calvary. How could anyone be saved by just enduring?

In these words, spoken by Christ, *saved* and *endure* have a different meaning than normal usage. Christ is speaking directly to the Jews, and He is not simply speaking of redemption and faith. He is looking far into the future when all of Israel who are still alive when the 7th Bowl judgment is poured out will be saved by faith in Jesus Christ and not by the law. It would be a serious mistake to think that Jesus Christ is granting salvation based upon survival or endurance as the Age of Grace is nearing an end. Any other conclusion is in conflict with many New Testament passages of scripture. Salvation is not by works, endurance, patience and love but by the precious blood of Jesus Christ. He or she that *believes* that truth to the end…no matter when or how…will be saved.

And this gospel of the kingdom shall be preached in all the world for a witness unto all Nations; and then shall the end come   Matthew 24:14

This can be a confusing statement without proper context. Paul made the following statement.

If ye continue in the faith grounded and settled, and be not moved away from the hope of the gospel, which ye have heard, and **which was preached to every creature which is under heaven**; *whereof I Paul am made a minister*   Colossians 1:23

Paul wrote Colossians in the 1st century AD. At that time, the known world were those countries from England to the far east, Russia to the North, the Far East to the West, and Africa to the south. We understand from biblical and historical records that the 12 Apostles spread the gospel to all known Nations, and that without a doubt it was spread by mouth across the *known world*. We now know that the *world* is not flat but round and contains many more people than was known then. There may be people outside of the known world in the 1st century AD that have not heard the Gospel message.... but before this age comes to an end they will.

[6] And I saw another angel fly in the midst of heaven, having the everlasting gospel to preach unto them that dwell on the earth, and to every Nation, and kindred, and tongue, and people,
[7] Saying with a loud voice, Fear God, and give glory to him; for the hour of his judgment is come: and worship him that made heaven, and earth, and the sea, and the fountains of waters   Revelation 14: 6-7

Until that time, it is the responsibility of every Christian to spread the Gospel message to all we can.......in every town, state and Nation.

> *For then shall be great tribulation, such as was not since the beginning of the world to this time, no, nor ever shall be*   Matthew 24:21

Jesus Christ now starts to describe a *sign* which will be given that a period of Great Tribulation is about to begin. Interestingly, the key to understanding the remainder of the Olivet Discourse is found in the prophetic Book of Daniel. Daniel is the cornerstone of all prophecy revealed in Matthew 24:14 - Matthew 25:46. The Book of Daniel and the Book of Revelation stand as bookends to all Old Testament and New Testament prophecies.

Authors Comment: In Daniel Chapter 2 the prophet is shown a vision of a Giant colossus which represents the fate of the Nation Israel from the end of Babylonian Captivity until the end of the Church Age. It is a remarkable Revelation of what will happen to the Jews over the next 2500 years. The members of this statue represented  what would happen on the European stage as it pertained to the Jews. The image which Daniel saw resembled a man. It was composed of different types of metals. The *head* was of *Gold*, and represented the Babylonian Empire. The *chest and arms* were of *silver,* and represented the dual Medo-Persian Empire. The *belly and thighs* were *bronze* and represented the Macedonian-Greek empire. The *lower part of each leg* was *iron* and represented the Roman Empire which was divided into the Western and Eastern parts. Finally, the *feet* with 10-toes were composed of a mixture of *iron and clay.* The 10 toes repesented a final latter-day 10 Nation confederacy which would be formed from out of nations that were part of the old Roman Empire. These 10 nations have sometimes been called the *Revived Roman Empire*. Danial was shown this image and its meaning near the beginning of the 70 years of captivity by the Babylonian Empire. Each portion of this collosus represented an empire which would dominate and persecute Israel until the Church Age comes to an end. The image starts with a head of Gold and ends with feet made of a mixture of iron and clay.

Four of these great world empires have come and gone: The Babylonian, Medo-Persian, Greecian and the old Roman Empire. When Christ conducted His 3.5-year ministry in the 1st Century AD, almost all of the known world was a part of the Roman Empire. The united Roman Empire lasted over 500 years. In 286 AD it split into the Eastern and Western empires, each ruled by its own emperor. The Western Empire suffered several Gothic invasions, and it continued to decline until 476 AD when the Western Roman Empire came to an end. The division of the Old roman Empire represents how Europe will continue to be divided into two ideologies. The 10 toes were made of iron mixed with clay, which represented instability. Some of these 10 nations will be weak….others strong.

The Old Roman Empire splintered into most of the 44 European Nations that we know today. It will not be long until Biblical Prophecy will be fulfilled, and Europe will unite under a 10-Nation confederacy and a common currency. It is unknown how long this coalition of Nations will remain intact, but at some time in the future a powerful orator, staesman and military genius will arise from *among* the 10 Nation confederacy. He will attack and conquer 3 countries in the 10-Nation confederacy, and by supernatural power he will assume dictatorship over the entire European

Theatre (Daniel 7). As part of his supernatural power, he will enter into a Peace Treaty with Israel. He will manage to rebuild Herod's Temple and allow the Jews to resume temple worship in Jerusalem. This Peace Treaty and the Temple being rebuilt will move many Jews to assume that he is their long awaited messiah, but this will not last long. The Jews will be decieved for a season, and after a brief period of peace and stability, the Great Tribulation will begin and the 1st thing that Satan will do is to apparently kill the great leader with a knife or sword (Revelation 13: 3-4). Satan will then enter into the body of this great world leader, bring him back to life, and become the *Antichrist* (Revelation 13:8). Satan will then attack and conquer Jerusalem and the new Temple. This European dictator will turn upon Israel and the Peace Treaty will be called a *Covenant with Death*.

Incredibly, these end-time events were revealed to Daniel by the great collossus and by a series of visions which follow. Any serious student of prophecy should carefully study the Book of Daniel. The feet of iron and clay represent the political and militaty power of the final 10-Nation confederacy. Satan will rule over the entire world as the *Antichrist* from his throne in the Holy Place of the new temple. However, the severe persecution and torment of the Antichrist will only last for 3.5 years, which is the last half of Daniel's 70th and final week.

[**42**] *Jesus saith unto them, Did ye never read in the scriptures, The stone which the builders rejected, the same is become the head of the corner: this is the Lord's doing, and it is marvelous in our eyes?*
[**43**] *Therefore say I unto you, The kingdom of God shall be taken from you, and given to a Nation bringing forth the fruits thereof.*

[44] *And whosoever shall fall on this stone shall be broken: but on whomsoever it shall fall, it will grind him to powder*
Matthew 21: 41-42

Jesus Christ is the cornerstone that the builders rejected. the concept came from Psalms 118: 22-23. King David compares Jesus Christ to the cornerstone in Psalms 118. When Daniel finished interpreting the Colossus which represented how the Jews would be treated until Jesus comes again, he saw another vision in which a great stone rolled down a mountain and strike the two feet and 10 toes of the colossus (Daniel 2: 34-35).

[34] *Daniel gazed at the statue until a stone was cut out without hands, which smote the image upon his feet that were of iron and clay, and brake them to pieces.*
[35] *Then was the iron, the clay, the brass, the silver, and the gold, broken to pieces together, and became like the chaff of the summer threshing floors; and the wind carried them away, that no place was found for them: and* **the stone that smote the image became a great mountain, and filled the whole earth.**

There will only be one kingdom in the *Kingdom of God* (the 1000 Year millennial Kingdom), and one ruler of all the world……...Jesus Christ.

[1] *But in the last days it shall come to pass, that the mountain of the house of the LORD shall be established in the top of the mountains, and it shall be exalted above the hills; and people shall flow unto it.*
[2] *And many Nations shall come, and say, Come, and let us go up to the mountain of the LORD, and to the house of the God of Jacob; and he will teach us of his ways, and we will walk in his paths: for the law*

shall go forth of Zion, and the word of the LORD from Jerusalem.
[3] *And he shall judge among many people, and rebuke strong Nations afar off; and they shall beat their swords into plowshares, and their spears into pruninghooks: Nation shall not lift up a sword against Nation, neither shall they learn war any more.*   Micah 4: 1-3

To summarize these end-time events, the Great Tribulation of 3.5 years will be immrdiately preceded by a great heavenly conflict between Micheal and God's holy angels and Satan and his unholy angels. Satan will be defeated and cast out of the heavenly realm down to earth. This will infuriate Satan and He will then attempt to exterminate all Christians and Jews. (1) He will turn on the Inhabitants of Jerusalem who will flee to the the mountains of a wilderness….. possibly Petra. (2) Just as Satan is about to overtake the fleeing remnant, God will miraculously rescue them with what appears to be an earthquake and a great chasm. It is not clear exactly what will happen next, but: (3) The great European military genious will be killed by a knife or a sword (4) Satan will resurrect this man or raise him from near death, and inherit his body (5) This new man will be called the *Antichrist*. (5) Satan as the Antichrist will give rise to a False Prophet who will support the Antichrist. (6) The antichriast will attack and conquer Jerusalem, and he will establish his throne in the newly built temple and declare himself to be GOD

> **[15]** *When ye therefore shall see the **abomination of desolation, spoken of by Daniel the prophet**, stand in the holy place, (whoso readeth, let him understand:)*
> **[16]** ***Then let them which be in Judaea flee** into the mountains:*
> **[17]** *Let him which is on the housetop not come down to take anything out of his house:*
> **[18]** *Neither let him which is in the field return back to take his clothes.*
> **[19]** *And woe unto them that are with child, and to them that give suck in those days!*
> **[20]** *But pray ye that your flight be not in the winter, neither on the sabbath day:*
> **[21]** ***For then shall be great tribulation**, such as was not since the beginning of the world to this time, no, nor ever shall be*
> Matthew 24: 15-21

Orthodox Jews will probably witness on television the great heavenly conflict between Micheal and Satan, but they will likely not understand what is happening. However, when they learn that Satan and his angels are surrounding Jerusalem, they are told to flee for their lives. Satan in the form of the Antichrist will conquer Jerusalem and then sit in the rebuilt temple declaring himself to be God. Christ spoke of this abomination (Matthew 24:15), but the clearest description of this apostasy is by Paul.

[1] *Now we beseech you, brethren, by the **coming of our Lord Jesus Christ**, and by our gathering together unto him,*
[2] *That ye be not soon shaken in mind, or be troubled, neither by spirit, nor by word, nor by letter as from us, as that the day of Christ is at hand.*
[3] *Let no man deceive you by any means: for **that day shall not come**, except there come a falling away first, and that man of sin be revealed, the son of perdition;*
[4] *Who opposes and exalts himself above all that is called God, or that is worshipped; so that he as God sits in the temple of God, shewing himself that he is God.*   I Thessalonians 2: 1-4

Paul is very clear about four future events. (1) A Man of Sin (Satan as the Antichrist) will arise who will set in the Temple of God and declare himself to be worshipped as God (2) I Thessalonians 2:1 refers to the *rapture* of the saints (3) The rapture will not occur until the *Man of Sin* is revealed as an imposter (4) There will be a great falling away before the Man of Sin is revealed.

Jesus warns the Jews in Matthew 24: 15-21 that when they see Jerusalem being surrounded by the enemy, they should flee *immediately*. Do not look back…do not pack your clothes…do not delay one second. He warns that if any woman has a small child (*brephos*) then there will be great difficulty. The final warning is that this invasion will not be on Sunday, because Orthodox Jews cannot travel more than 2000 paces on a Sunday. Those who ignore these warnings will experience great danger.

There will be two invasions of Jerusalem by Satan during this period of great tribulation, and one immediately following the 1000-year Millennial Kingdom. The 1st is called the *Jerusalem Campaign*, and it will take place shortly after Satan is cast out of heaven. The 2nd will be called the *Armageddon Campaign,* and it will take place at the end of the tribulation period as Satan and his forces assemble to attack Jerusalem. This 3rd invasion will be called *Satan's Last Stand* and it will close the 1000-year *Millennial Kingdom*. The invasion of Jerusalem (Jerusalem Campaign) which initiates the *Wrath of Satan* is what Jesus Christ is describing in Matthew 24: 15-21. Christ never described the Battle of Armageddon or Satan's Last Stand in Matthew 24 or Matthew 25, this was revealed in Revelation 19: 1-21 and Revelation 20: 7-10.

When Satan breaks the Peace Treaty with Israel and invades Jerusalem, there will be a short but intense battle to conquer the city and occupy the newly rebuilt temple (The *Jerusalem Campaign*). The prophet Zachariah seems to prophecy of how many Jews will be killed during the Jerusalem Campaign *and* the Great Tribulation.

[7] Awake, O sword, against my shepherd, and against the man that is my fellow, saith the LORD of hosts: smite the shepherd, and the sheep shall be scattered: and I will turn mine hand upon the little ones.
[8] And it shall come to pass, that in all the land, saith the LORD, **two parts therein shall be cut off and die; but the third shall be left therein.**
[9] And I will bring the third part through the fire, and will refine them as silver is refined, and will try them as gold is tried: they shall call on my name, and I will hear them: I will say, It is my people: and they shall say, The LORD is my God.
  Zachariah 13: 7-9

Zachariah prophesies that 2/3 of the inhabitants of Jerusalem will be killed. Some identify Zachariah 13:8 as a prophecy which applies to the destruction of Jerusalem in either 586 BC or in 70 AD, but this is incorrect. 2/3 of all Israel will be killed during the Great Tribulation.

In Matthew 24: 1-20, Christ has spoken of things which will precede or characterize the Great Tribulation. He now turns to describe the Great Tribulation itself.

Chapter 4

The Great Tribulation Begins

> [21] *For then shall be great tribulation, such as was not since the beginning of the world to this time, no, nor ever shall be.*
> [22] *And except those days should be shortened, there should no flesh be saved: but for the elect's sake those days shall be shortened*
> Matthew 24: 21-22

Christ warns His apostles (and anyone who would read Matthew 24: 21-22) that a tribulation more severe than any that had ever occurred since the world began would take place in the future. He also spoke of general conditions which will intensify prior to when Great Tribulation starts (Matthew 24: 4-7), Christ gave no indication of how long it would be until he returned. The only thing that He consistently taught is: *be ready* and *watchful*. From the Book of Revelation and from the prophet Daniel, we know that this time of great prosecution will be a *time, time and half-a-time* or about 3.5 years. It will begin after Satan is cast out of heaven and will end at the Battle of Armageddon. As previously discussed, some biblical researchers teach that the Olivet Discourse was describing the fall of Jerusalem and Herod's Temple in 70 AD. The things described in Matthew 24 never predicted when the Temple would be destroyed, and in 70 AD the people of Jerusalem were captured and scattered throughout the Roman Empire. However, they are wrong. The devastation and destruction in 70 AD were terrible, but it was local to Israel and Jerusalem.

The great Jewish historian Flavius Josephus, who was there, wrote that the Temple was burned to the ground and not one stone remained in place. The heroic defenders locked themselves inside, and without food or water, they fought to the death. The horrible devastation and death of all who were outside the temple was equally terrible. One story was about a Jewish woman who killed her only daughter and ate her rather than surrender.

The events described by Jesus Christ in Matthew 24 predict a *Great Tribulation* that the *world* had never seen before and would never experience again. Christ then makes an astounding statement: *These days of great persecution will be shortened for His elect.* Jesus is looking far into the future and the end of the Age. This does not mean that the last half of Daniel's 70th week will be cut short….it must run its full course. It means that the *elect* will be spared from part of the great tribulation…the last part. *What is the last part?* I believe that this means that all born-again, true believers will be spared from that portion of the last 3.5 years which is called the *Wrath of God* which are the *7 Bowl Judgments* (Revelation 15:1, Revelation 16:1*). All* born-again Christians are promised that they would not experience the Wrath of God.

For the Wrath of God is revealed from heaven against all ungodliness and unrighteousness of men, who hold the truth in unrighteousness Romans 1:18

Much more then, being now justified by his blood, we shall be saved from wrath through him   Romans 5:9

For God hath not appointed us to wrath, but to obtain salvation by our Lord Jesus Christ   I Thessalonians 5:9

Can we absolutely determine what is the Wrath of God?... Yes, we can.

[1] *And I saw another sign in heaven, great and marvelous, seven angels having the seven last plagues; for in them is filled up the* **Wrath of God**.

[7] *And one of the four beasts gave unto the seven angels seven golden vials full of the* **Wrath of God***, who lives for ever and ever*
Revelation 15: 1,7

*And I heard a great voice out of the temple saying to the seven angels: Go your ways, and pour out the vials of the **Wrath of God** upon the earth*   Revelation 16:1

The Wrath of God is without controversy the 7 Bowl or Vial Judgments. Now consider what happens when the 7th Trumpet is sounded.

*[15] **And the seventh angel sounded**; and there were great voices in heaven, saying, The kingdoms of this world are become the kingdoms of our Lord, and of his Christ; and he shall reign for ever and ever.*
[16] And the four and twenty elders, which sat before God on their seats, fell upon their faces, and worshipped God,
[17] Saying, We give thee thanks, O Lord God Almighty, which art, and wast, and art to come; because thou hast taken to thee thy great power, and hast reigned.
*[18] And the nations were angry, **and thy Wrath is come**, and **the time of the dead, that they should be judged, and that thou shouldest give reward unto thy servants the prophets, and to the saints**, and them that fear thy name, small and great; and shouldest destroy them which destroy the earth.*   Revelation 11: 15-18

Revelation 11:15 and Revelation 11:18 clearly state that when the 7th Trumpet sounds: **The Wrath of God is come.** Putting all of the pieces together: (1) All born-again believers (John 3:3) are promised that they would not experience the *Wrath of God.* (2) The Wrath of God are the 7 Bowl Judgments. If all born-again Christians (Jews and Gentiles) are not destined to go through the 7 Bowl Judgments in the Book of Revelation, then this clearly implies that they will not be around when the Wrath of God falls upon all unbelievers. Now look at Revelation 11:18 again.

*And the nations were angry, **and thy Wrath is come**, and **the time of the dead**, that **they should be judged**, and that thou shouldest **give reward unto thy servants the prophets, and to the saints**, and them that fear thy name, small and great; and shouldest **destroy them which destroy the earth***   Revelation 11:18

Without any preconceived bias, anyone should recognize that this is the Rapture of the Saints (elect). Paul said:

*[16] For the Lord himself shall descend from heaven with a shout, with the voice of the archangel, and **with the trump of God**: and the dead in Christ shall rise first:*
[17] Then we which are alive and remain shall be caught up together with them in the clouds, to meet the Lord in the air: and so shall we ever be with the Lord   I Thessalonians 4:17

Jesus said:

> *And he shall send his angels with a great sound of a **trumpet**, and they shall gather together his elect from the four winds, from one end of heaven to the other*   Matthew 24:31

Paul is more specific about which trump.

[51] Behold, I shew you a mystery; We shall not all sleep, but we shall all be changed,
*[52] In a moment, in the twinkling of an eye, **at the last trump**: for the trumpet shall sound, and the dead shall be raised incorruptible, and we shall be changed*   I Corinthians 15: 51-62

Piecing all of this together: The Rapture of the church will take place as the last (7th Trumpet) sounds. If the reader needs more convincing, this Biblical Truth is completely developed and presented in Phillips, *A New Pre-Wrath Rapture Theory*.

The following discussion has been included to add clarity and context to the *Olivet Discourse*.

The entire Daniel 70-week prophecy is Jewish and concerns a period of time when God is dealing with the Jews (490 years). Jesus Christ was born a Jew, lived as a Jew and died as a Jew. He lived a sinless and perfect life under the Old Covenant, and He offered Himself as the perfect sacrificial lamb of God. he established a *New Covenant* so that the *Old Covenant* of salvation by works could be replaced by a new and better New Covenant based upon faith and grace.

Christ lived every day of His ministry as a Jew under the ancient Jewish calendar that was in use at least since the Exodus from Egypt and possibly before that time. It is only necessary to observe that the Jewish lunar calendar was well established by the 1st century AD, and it is still in use today. It is adjusted yearly to keep the Lunar year in sync with the solar year, and over a 19-year period (called a Metonic Cycle), it almost exactly matches the modern Gregorian Solar Calendar. The Jewish lunar calendar is remarkable in that it is designed to start every month on a new moon, and at the same time accurately track the seasons. Modern computer scientists and NASA have constructed calendar conversion programs to match each Jewish calendar date and day to the corresponding Gregorian calendar over thousands of years. The results used in this section of the book are generated by a program called *Abdicate*, which has been verified by a 3rd party software (HEBCAL) and available NASA documents.

The Hebrew lunar/solar Calendar was in use by the Jews during the Babylonian captivity, it is in use today, and it will be in use during the (future) reign of Satan during the Great Tribulation. In the following calculations, there is no reason to use either the Gregorian Calendar or the Roman calendar at all, although in the 1st Century AD the Roman Calendar was in use throughout the Roman Empire. The Jewish Calendar was maintained and used by the Jews to schedule the 7 Feasts of Israel and the Jewish Holy Days according to Gods instructions. We need to know that Jesus Christ was Crucified on the *Feast of Passover*, Nisan 14, on a Wednesday in 30 AD (Phillips, *The Birth and Death of Christ*). The *4 Spring Feasts of Israel* (Feast of Passover, Feast of Unleavened Bread, Feast of Firstfruits and the Feast of Pentecost) were completely satisfied by Jesus Christ at His 1st coming, and the *3 Fall*

Feasts (Feast of Trumpets, Feast of Yom Kippur and the Feast of Tabernacles will be completely satisfied by Jesus Christ at His 2nd advent (Phillips, *The 7 Feasts of Israel*). The following observations have previously been determined in: (Phillips, *A New Pre-Wrath Rapture* and Phillips: The Birth of Christ: *A Forensic Analysis*).

- Christ was crucified on the 1st day of the *Feast of Passover*; Wednesday, Nisan 14 in 30 AD
- His earthly ministry was 3.5 years in duration
- The rapture of all saints will occur on the *Feast of Trumpets* (Tishri 1)
- The Battle of Armageddon will take place on the *Feast of Yom Kippur* (Tishri 10)
- The *Feast of Tabernacles* (Tishri 15- Tishri 22) will immediately precede the 1000-year Millennial Kingdom
- When Satan and his fallen angels are cast out of heaven (Revelation 12: 7-9), the Great Tribulation will begin which will contain the 7 Trumpet Judgments (*Wrath of Satan*...Revelation 12:12) and the 7 Bowl Judgments (*Wrath of God*...Revelation 15:1, Revelation 16:1).
- The Great Tribulation will last a *times, time and half-a-time*...3.5 years (Daniel 7:25, Daniel 12:7, Revelation 12:14).

It is interesting that the vast majority of prophecy teachers and students believe that the Tribulation will be 7 years in duration. It has been shown that this is based upon non-biblical reasoning in Phillips, *A New Pre-Wrath Rapture Theory*, but regardless of what anyone might choose to believe we will only be concerned with the last 3.5 years of the Great Tribulation, and Christ only spoke of that time period in His Olivet discourse except when He described General Conditions that would precede the *Great Tribulation*.

The majority of prophecy teachers insist that the duration of the Great Tribulation is 7 years. This is incorrect and should be rejected. The reason that this cannot be true is that the 7 Seal Judgments *do not* sequentially precede the 7 Trumpet Judgments and the 7 Bowl Judgments in lock-step sequence. This is proved in Phillips, *A New Pre-Wrath Rapture Theory*.

The New Covenant based upon faith and grace was not initiated until Christ died for the sins of the world on the Cross of Calvary. If the Daniel 70-Week Prophecy started with an edict issued to Ezra the Scribe in September of 458 BC (Phillips, *The 70 Week Prophecy of Daniel* and Phillips, *A Forensic Analysis of the Birth and Death of Jesus Christ*), the 3.5-year ministry of Christ would have begun in the Spring of 26 AD, 483 years later (Note one year must be subtracted when passing from 1 BC to 1 AD). This would leave 7 years in the Daniel 490 Year Prophecy. Christ taught and healed for 3.5 years and died in the Fall of 30 AD, half-way through the last 7 years of the Daniel prophecy. These 3.5 years for the earthly ministry of Jesus Christ were to the Jews and *must* be part of the Daniel Prophecy. The suspension (gap) in the Daniel Prophecy cannot begin until *after* Christ was crucified. This leaves exactly a *time-times-and half a time* (3.5 years) for the *Wrath of Satan* (7 Trumpet Judgments) and the *Wrath of God* (7 Bowl Judgments). This is precisely what should happen. Although seldom stated, some biblical researchers have suspended the Daniel Prophecy when Christ *began* His ministry, and they have proposed that the 490-year prophecy of Daniel be interrupted when Christ *began* His earthly ministry. This is impossible and should be rejected.

Using different sets of assumptions, biblical scholars have determined that from when the 490-year prophecy began and the crucifixion of Christ was 483 years. This would leave *7 years* for the *Great Tribulation*. This author has devoted a great deal of research analyzing all positions, and based upon available archeological evidence and the Holy Scriptures propose that the Daniel 70-Week prophecy started in the fall of 448 BC in the 7th Regnal year of King Nebuchadnezzar

(September 1, 448 BC-September 1, 447 BC, and was suspended (interrupted) in the Spring of 30 AD when Christ was crucified. This would leave 3.5 years for the Great Tribulation. Nothing is strained and everything falls into place at it should. The Daniel prophecy was suspended in the Spring of 30 BC when God and His Son Jesus Christ turned to the Gentiles. This created a *Gap* of almost 2000 years (30 AD-2024 AD) as this book is written. This is called the *Gap Theory* by modern prophecy teachers. The 490-Year prophecy of Daniel will not resume until the Great Tribulation begins.

The sequence of events which will take place during the last 3.5 years of the Great Tribulation is summarized in the following diagram. This graphic only illustrates the main events which will take place after Satan is cast down to earth in Revelation 12. The last 3 Fall Feasts of the 7 Feasts of Israel are identified with: (1) The Rapture of the Saints-The *Feast of Trumpets* (2) The Battle of Armageddon-The *Feast of Yom Kippur* and (3) The Wedding Supper of the Lamb-Feast of Tabernacles

The 7 holy Feasts of Israel provide a *blueprint* of major events Phillips, *The 7 Feasts of Israel*). This diagram only illustrates the chronological

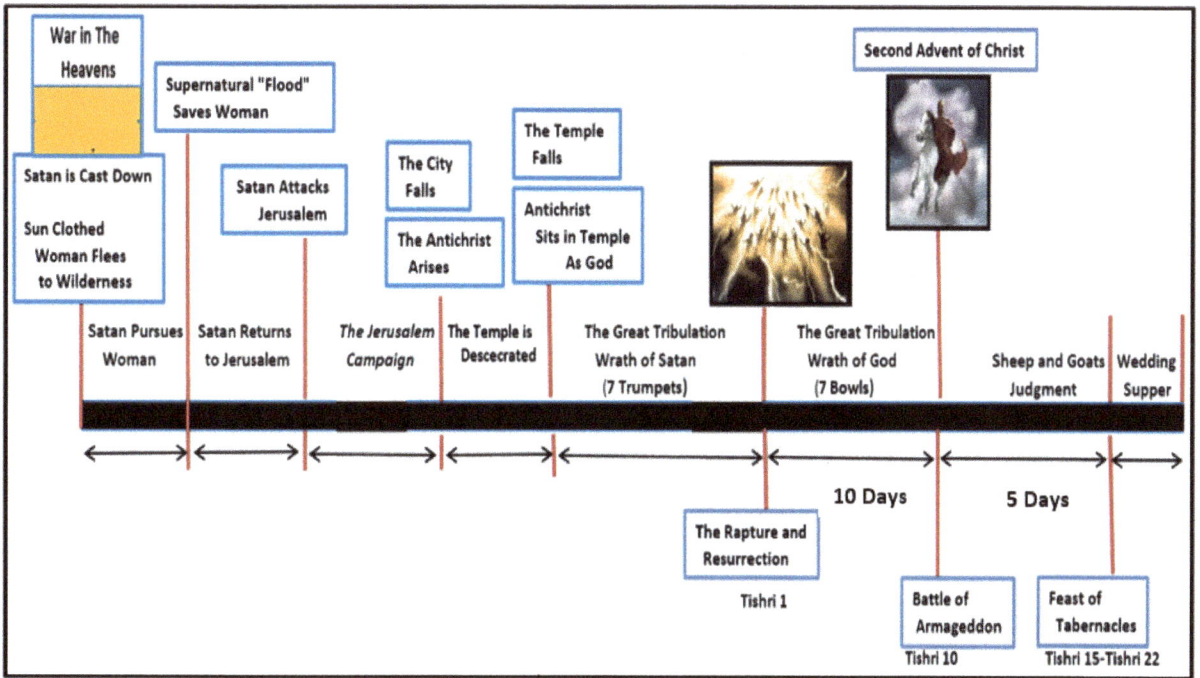

sequence of selected key events which will take place in the last half of Daniel's 70th Week.

> [23] *Then if any man shall say unto you, Lo: Here is Christ, or there: believe it not.*
> [24] *For there shall arise false Christs, and false prophets, and shall shew great signs and wonders; deceive the very elect. Insomuch that, if it were possible, they shall deceive the very elect.*
> [25] *Behold, I have told you before*
> [26] *Wherefore if they shall say unto you, Behold, he is in the desert; go not forth: behold, he is in the secret chambers; believe it not.*
> [27] *For as the lightning cometh out of the east, and shineth even unto the west, so shall also the coming of the Son of man be*
> [28] *For wheresoever the carcass is, there will the eagles be gathered together.*   Matthew 24: 23-28

The words of Jesus Christ in Matthew 24: 23-27 should be read in the proper context. Christ is assuming that all born-again Christians will eagerly be awaiting the 2nd advent of Jesus Christ, and that they will be looking for signs. This is what the apostles wanted Jesus Christ to explain as they asked: *what shall be the sign of thy coming?* (Matthew 24:3). Christ had already warned them that:

> [5] *For many shall come in my name, saying, I am Christ; and shall deceive many.*
> [6] *And ye shall hear of wars and rumors of wars: see that ye be not troubled: for all these things must come to pass, but the end is not yet.*
> [7] *For nation shall rise against nation, and kingdom against kingdom: and there shall be famines, and pestilences, and earthquakes, in divers places*   Matthew 24: 5-7

If someone comes to you and declares that Christ has finally come back, do not believe them. Paul informed us that the second advent of Christ will be in two parts: *First*, He will appear suddenly and boldly, in the sight of everyone, to call all of His elect to him to meet him in the air. This is the *Rapture. Second*, Christ will come down to the earth to fight the *Battle of Armageddon* against all unbelievers 10 days later. This will not be a surprise and both will take place with heavenly signs (Revelation 11: 18-19, Revelation 16: 15-21).

In the last two centuries there have been terrible wars fought: WWI, WWII, Korean, Vietnam, Etc.) but these did not end this current age. Christ said that these things are to be expected but the end *is not yet*. Television evangelists and news networks around the world will report earthquakes, floods, famines and wars; but these things must take place before the Great Tribulation begins.

The Antichrist will rise from death or near-death to be the earthly dwelling of Satan (Revelation 13: 1-9). Satan will fabricate and erect statues of himself that will speak and demand that Satan as the Antichrist be worshipped as God (Revelation 13:15). Satan will desecrate the Holy Temple in Jerusalem (Revelation 11: 1-2), and He will wield such power that no one can buy or sell without his mark on their wrist or forehead (Revelation 13: 16-17). There will be powerful antichrists who speak for Satan and eloquent false prophets that will kill, maim, destroy and preach false salvation (Matthew 24:5). Jesus warned that these evil men would deceive His *very elect* if it were possible without the Holy Spirit to guide them and interpret truth (Matthew 24:24). Christ will come suddenly for His elect (rapture): It will happen quickly and will come as lightning can be seen across the sky from East to West (Matthew 24:27). Jesus Christ then spoke what must have been a very confusing revelation.

> *For wheresoever the carcass is, there will the eagles be gathered together*   Matthew 24:28

In the Book of Revelation this strange prophecy is fulfilled. After Christ has returned to fight the Battle of Armageddon, the following was written by John.

[17] And I saw an angel standing in the sun; and he cried with a loud voice, saying to all the fowls that fly in the midst of heaven, Come and gather yourselves together unto the supper of the great God;
[18] That ye may eat the flesh of kings, and the flesh of captains, and the flesh of mighty men, and the flesh of horses, and of them that sit on them, and the flesh of all men, both free and bond, both small and great
Revelation 19: 17-18

This is obviously the aftermath of Matthew 24: 29-31.

> [29] **Immediately after the tribulation of those days** *shall the sun be darkened, and the moon shall not give her light, and the stars shall fall from heaven, and the powers of the heavens shall be shaken:*
> [30] *And then shall appear* **the sign** *of the Son of man in heaven: and then shall all the tribes of the earth mourn, and they shall see the Son of man coming in the clouds of heaven with power and great glory.*
> [31] *And he shall send his angels with a great sound of a trumpet, and they shall* **gather together his elect** *from the four winds, from one end of heaven to the other*   Matthew 24: 29-31

This is also the answer that Jesus Christ gave to His apostles concerning *when shall these things be?* (Matthew 24:3, Matthew 24:29).

The apostles knew little of the details concerning *when shall Christ return.* Since they asked the question in Matthew 24:3, we have the benefit of what has been written for us concerning the answer by the Books of the New Testament in English, the 13 epistles of Paul and the Book of Revelation which was penned by John. We now know that the second advent of Christ will be in two phases. The 1st is when He returns in the air to gather all born-again believers (alive and dead) to him. The 2nd will be when Jesus Christ returns to this earth to fight the Battle of Armageddon. The apostles knew nothing concerning both of these events. In fact, they probably believed that Christ would immediately or very shortly establish His Kingdom here on earth. They certainly knew none of the details concerning the Church Age and the New Covenant by which salvation is offered by faith and grace to Jews and Gentiles alike. Nevertheless, to Jesus Christ *one day is like 1000 years* and He told them things which only made sense after the entire New Testament was written. However, in Matthew 24: 29-31 Christ revealed several revealing and extremely important prophecies.

- Christ will not appear again until **after** the Tribulation of these days.
- There will be **signs** in the earth and in the heavens that Christ is about to return (The sun will go dark, the moon will not shine, stars will fall from the sky, and the other planets in our galaxy will shake.
- After these signs **then the Son of Man** (Jesus Christ) will appear in the heavenlies.
- Everyone will **see** this happen
- Christ will send His angels to **bring all of His *elect*** to Him *in the air* from *all over* the earth.
- The **dead in Christ** will rise first, and then **those who are alive** and ready to meet Him.

As I speak to different individuals and churches, there is one question which is always asked: *When will the rapture take place*? This question always amazes me, and I ask if they have read and understood what Christ said in Matthew 24? Christ was very specific about several key points

- The Rapture and resurrection of all born-again believers will not occur until ***after*** the *Tribulation*. It will not be *before* or in the *middle*, but *after*. Note that He did not say after the *Great Tribulation*. The Great Tribulation is a modern term composed of two separate parts: The 7 Trumpet judgments (Wrath and tribulation of Satan) and the 7 Bowl Judgments (Bowls of Wrath of God. Christians are not destined to experience the Wrath of God, and the Wrath of God is the 7 Bowl Judgments (carefully read Revelation 11: 15-19, Revelation 11:8 and particularly, Revelation 15:1 and Revelation 16:1)

[2] *In my Father's house are many mansions: if it were not so, I would have told you. I go to prepare a place for you.*
[3] *And if I go and prepare a place for you,* **I will come again, and receive you unto myself**; *that where I am, there ye may be also*
John 14: 2-3

The rapture will not occur until after Satan is cast out of heaven, he declares himself to be God, he sits in the temple in Jerusalem and after the 7th Trumpet has sounded (Phillips, *A New Pre-Wrath Rapture Theory*)

[1] *Now we beseech you, brethren, by the coming of our Lord Jesus Christ, and by our gathering together unto him,*
[2] *That ye be not soon shaken in mind, or be troubled, neither by spirit, nor by word, nor by letter as from us, as that the day of Christ is at hand.*
[3] *Let no man deceive you by any means: for* **that day shall not come**, *except there come a falling away first, and that* **man of sin be revealed,** *the son of perdition;*
[4] *Who opposes and exalts himself above all that is called God, or that is worshipped; so that he as God* **sits in the temple of God, shewing himself that he is God.**
[5] *Remember ye not, that, when I was yet with you, I told you these things?*
[6] *And now ye know what withholds that he might be revealed in his time.*
[7] *For the mystery of iniquity doth already work: only he who now lets will let, until he be taken out of the way.*
[8] *And then shall that Wicked be revealed, whom the Lord shall*

consume with the spirit of his mouth, and shall destroy with the brightness of his coming   II Thessalonians 2: 1-8

Paul revealed more details about the rapture in I Thessalonians 4.

[16] *For **the Lord himself shall descend from heaven** with a shout, with the voice of the archangel, and **with the trump of God**: and the dead in Christ shall rise first:*
[17] *Then we which are alive and remain shall be caught up together with them in the clouds, to meet the Lord in the air: and so shall we ever be with the Lord*   I Thessalonians 4: 16-17

Paul is then more specific in his letter to Corinth concerning the trump of God.

[51] *Behold, **I shew you a mystery**; We shall not all sleep, but we shall all be changed,*
[52] *In a moment, in the twinkling of an eye, **at the last trump**: for the trumpet shall sound, and the dead shall be raised incorruptible, and we shall be changed.*
[53] *For this corruptible must put on incorruption, and this mortal must put on immortality.*
[54] *So when this corruptible shall have put on incorruption, and this mortal shall have put on immortality, then shall be brought to pass the saying that is written, Death is swallowed up in victory*
I Corinthians 15: 51-54

In his letter to Corinth, Paul identifies the trump which will be sounded to call the elect upward…. It is the *last trump*.

Chapter 5
What Will Be the Sign of Thy Coming?

Christ does not set a timeline for His return. Instead, he speaks of how one would know as the end draws near. Christ uses a short parable which refers to a *fig tree* (John 15:5, Romans 11: 17-24).

The Parable of the Fig Tree

> [32] *Now learn a parable of the fig tree; When his branch is yet tender, and puts forth leaves, ye know that summer is nigh:*
> [33] *So likewise ye, when ye shall see all these things, know that it is near, even at the doors.*
> [34] *Verily I say unto you: This generation shall not pass, till all these things be fulfilled.*
> [35] *Heaven and earth shall pass away, but my words shall not pass away*   Matthew 24: 32-35

Israel is often compared to a fig tree, and Christians are typed as *branches* which have been grafted into the main trunk. The *roots* of this

tree are *God* who sustains all things and has chosen Israel as His Holy Nation. The *trunk* of this tree which receives nourishment from the roots is the Nation of Israel. It would have been a mighty and lofty tree among all nations, but because of disobedience and apostasy it *never bore fruit* (Luke 3:9, Matthew 7:19). The branches still were sustained through the tap root, but they were only symbols of what God had chosen them to be. Because they never bore any fruit, God *cut them off* and *grafted* in another set of branches (Gentiles) who would grow His body, the Church (Romans 11: 11-24). As time went by, His body of New

Covenant Christians faltered also, but there were many branches that grew straight and bore fruit. Those who were called *Christians* (Acts 11:26), coexisted in an evil world with unbelievers. Like the wheat and tares, they both grew together and became almost indistinguishable from one another. The apostles recognized that some were Wheat and some were Tares, and suggested to Christ that the tares be removed from the field (earth), leaving only the precious fruit of born-again believers. But Christ said *No*, let them all grow together until the harvest, because if the tares are pulled up it might damage the precious wheat (Matthew 13: 24-33). So it is, that as the end of the age draws near the tares continue to multiply and grow. Like Bermuda grass and St. Augustine grass, they coexist, even though Bermuda grass is hearty and will rob nourishment from the soil. Today (2023) it would seem in the United States that the tares are choking out the wheat. Church attendance is in decline, young people are turning their back on God, abortion, demonstrations…WOKE and transgender/ unisex/homosexual "love" seems to be taking over. However, those born-again Christian who will remain faithful to the end will conquer death and Satan. Those who are grounded in the Word of God recognize that this is prophesied to precede the end of the age.

[1] *This know also, that **in the last days perilous times shall come**.*
[2] *For men shall be lovers of their own selves, covetous, boasters, proud, blasphemers, disobedient to parents, unthankful, unholy,*
[3] ***Without natural affection**, trucebreakers, false accusers, incontinent, fierce, despisers of those that are good,*
[4] *Traitors, heady, high-minded, lovers of pleasures more than lovers of God;*
[5] *Having a form of godliness, but denying the power thereof: from such turn away.*
[6] *For of this sort are they which creep into houses, and lead captive silly women laden with sins, led away with divers lusts,*
[7] *Ever learning, and never able to come to the knowledge of the truth.*
II Timothy 3: 1-7

Christ told His disciples (and us) that when these things start to come to pass, then be watchful…. for *the end is near, even at the door.* Christ then spoke of something which has caused a great deal of dissent and confusion in the body of Christ.

> *Verily I say unto you: This **generation** shall not pass, till all these things be fulfilled*   Matthew 24:34

Literal bible translators have used this as a *proof verse* that the entire Olivet Discourse applied to the destruction of Herod's Temple and the City of Jerusalem in 70 AD by Titus and his Roman army. In examining the entire context and content of Matthew 24, it is clear that this cannot be true. The Greek word for *generation* is *genea,* which can also be translated as *race*. The Jews have never been exterminated and Israel currently exists as a nation. The *race* of Israel is the correct translation from the Greek.

> *[36] But of that day and hour knoweth no man, no, not the angels of heaven, but my Father only.*
> *[37] But as the days of Noe were, so shall also the coming of the Son of man be.*
> *[38] For as in the days that were before the flood they were eating and drinking, marrying and giving in marriage, until the day that Noe entered into the ark,*
> *[39] And knew not until the flood came, and took them all away; so shall also the coming of the Son of man be*   Matthew 24: 36-39

Christ compares His 2nd coming to the Great flood of Noah's day.

Before the flood came and destroyed all but eight righteous people, the rest of the human race were marrying, drinking and partying. These activities will not condemn anyone to death or eternal damnation. There is nothing wrong with a glass of wine or a night out periodically. Jesus is not condemning these activities, but He is simply saying that when He comes again there will be many people who are not watching and waiting, but they will be carrying on as usual. This also does not say that they were not warned. Those who *missed the boat* saw the ark being built and simply laughed at Noah as if he was crazy. Before the great flood came, the people were warned about the devastating destruction for over 120 years (Genesis 6:3). They were *unconcerned* until the day that it started to rain, and as the deluge intensified the *flood came and swept them all away*. Nothing at all was said about sinful behavior in spite of what many teach, but that the warnings and signs were ignored, and when the rains came it was sudden and unexpected. They saw the ark as it neared completion, they saw the animals being loaded into the ark and they saw the storm clouds gathering. They were simply ignoring the immediate signs and carried on as usual. This is what will happen when Christ returns again.

It is a serious mistake to view the behavior of unbelievers as a sign that the end of the age is near. Not one word is said in this passage of scripture about sinful behavior. How does this support the biblical teaching of *surprise* and *immanency*? It does not.

Every Christian is told repeatedly to *watch* and *wait*, but not because the 2nd advent of Christ will be a total surprise. The event which will cause the *Great Tribulation* to begin will be the great heavenly conflict of Revelation 12. There will be no immediate signs that this is about to take place, but this is about 3.5 years before the end of the church age. There will be multiple signs that the end is near before Christ returns. (1) A 10-nation confederacy will unite and rule Europe. (2) A great orator and military leader will arise among the 10 nations, and attack and defeat 3 of the 10 nations (3) This great world leader, orator and military genius will then assume control of Europe as sole dictator. (4) This dictator will unify the European Theatre and sign a *Peacy Treaty* with Israel, called the *Covenant with Death*. (5) As part of this peace treaty, he will manage to rebuild the Jewish Temple in Jerusalem.

These will be visible signs that the Great Tribulation is near, very near. But according to Timothy most people will abandon the faith, become roaming beasts of protest and destruction, seek love with *strange flesh* and desire unnatural affection as these end-time events happen. As in the days before the flood, people will only love themselves, and live with no purpose in life like foaming waves of destruction.

> And knew not until the flood came, and took them all away; so shall also the coming of the Son of man be   Matthew 24:39

Christ will return, but these things must first come to pass. Christ now turns His comments to what we call the *rapture.*

> [40] Then shall two be in the field; the one shall be taken, and the other left.
> [41] Two women shall be grinding at the mill; the one shall be taken, and the other left.
> [42] Watch therefore: for ye know not what hour your Lord doth come.
> Matthew 24: 40-42

Authors Comment: Jesus Christ will return a 2nd time in what is called His *Second Advent*. The Second advent of Christ will take place in *two different phases*. The **1st Phase** will be when He will return in the air to gather to Him all of those who have died in Christ. The dead will rise 1st to meet Him in the air, and they will be followed by all who remain alive. This is called the *Rapture*. Immediately following the rapture, there will be no living true believer left upon the face of the earth. When this will take place is the subject of much theological debate. There are five main theological positions: (1) A *Pre-Tribulation* rapture which will take place 7 years before the Church Age is over (2) A *Mid-Tribulation* rapture which will take place when Satan is cast down to earth. This will usually take place 3.5 years before the Church Age is over. Some teach that the tribulation is 7-years long, but the rapture will not take place until 3.5 years have elapsed. (3) A *Post-*

Tribulation rapture which takes place at the end of a 7-year tribulation. The saints are raptured out and then immediately return to fight the Battle of Armageddon with Christ. A Post-Tribulation rapture was taught by the early church fathers, but due to multiple theological difficulties, it is rarely taught today. (4) A *Pre-Wrath* rapture which will take place as the 6th Seal is removed by Jesus Christ. This Pre-Wrath rapture assumes a 7-year tribulation period (5) A *Pre Wrath Rapture* which will take place on the Jewish *Feast of Trumpets*. This Pre-Wrath rapture assumes a 3.5-year period of tribulation. Each of these positions are covered in some detail in the book by Phillips, *A New Pre-Wrath Rapture Theory.* The **2nd Phase** will be when Christ will return to stand on this earth to fight the *Battle of Armageddon*. On that day, Christ will *descend* from Heaven to the *Mount of Olives,* which was where He *ascended* to Heaven after His resurrection and glorification. After He fights the Battle of Armageddon, He will remain on earth to rule and reign over Israel during the 1000-year Millennial Kingdom (See Phillips, *Life After the Great Tribulation*) from His Throne of Glory just north of Jerusalem.

The word *rapture* does not appear in the Holy Scriptures. It is a man-made term which comes from the Latin word *Raptura* which means to be *snatched away*. Jesus Christ does not examine any rapture position but He does refer to such an event

> *[40] Then shall two be in the field; the one shall be taken, and the other left.*
> *[41] Two women shall be grinding at the mill; the one shall be taken, and the other left.*
> *[42] Watch therefore: for ye know not what hour your Lord doth come.*
> *[43] But know this, that if the goodman of the house had known in what watch the thief would come, he would have watched, and would not have suffered his house to be broken up.*
> *[44] Therefore be ye also ready: for in such an hour as ye think not the Son of man cometh*   Matthew 24: 40-44

Paul was chosen by God to reveal the *Mystery* of a *rapture* (I Corinthians 15:50–54, 1 Thessalonians 4:16–17), but he did not predict exactly when it would take place.

In what was undoubtedly a confusing statement to His Apostles, Jesus said that on some day in the future: two people will be in the field; *one would be taken and one would be left*. Two people would be grinding grain at a mill and *one would be taken and one would be left*. This *must* refer to what we call the *rapture*. It does not imply that there will be a great separation of sinful people from Christians here on earth before the Great Tribulation begins. The proper interpretation of Christ words is identical to the *Parable of the Wheat and Tares* (Matthew 13: 36-43). In that parable Jesus Christ contrasts believers from unbelievers in the *world*. As the Church Age progresses, there will be unbelievers (tares) existing side-by-side with believers (wheat). The *field* is specifically identified as the *world*, and *Christ* is the *sower of good seed*. In ancient times, it was easy to corrupt the quality of a good field. An enemy or competitor would come and plant Tares in the good field. The *enemy* is *Satan*. Those who work and toil in the field would like to uproot and burn the tares as they grow among the wheat. But Jesus said *No*, lest you uproot and destroy the precious wheat. Christ said to let both grow together until the *harvest*, then separate the wheat from the tares and burn the tares. The reapers are the *angels* and the *harvest* will be at the *end of the World* (Matthew 13: 39-49).

> ***Authors Comment***: Christ said: *the tares are gathered and burned in the fire: So shall it be in the end of this world* (Matthew 13:40). Jesus revealed in the Olivet Discourse that all true believers would be gathered from the 4 corners of the world by *angels* (Matthew 24:31), and Paul said it would be at the sound of a *trump* (I Thessalonians 4:16) … the *last trump* (I Corinthians 15:52). All that will remain after the rapture will be unbelievers. After the 7 Bowls of God's Wrath are poured out,

the *tares* (unbelievers) will be gathered together to the Battle of Armageddon) and then they will all be cast into the Lake of Burning Fire (Revelation 19:20). A companion passage of scripture to Matthew 24: 40-41 is found in Luke 17: 34-36.

[34] *I tell you, in that night there shall be two men in one bed; the one shall be taken, and the other shall be left.*
[35] *Two women shall be grinding together; the one shall be taken, and the other left.*
[36] *Two men shall be in the field; the one shall be taken, and the other left*   Luke 17: 34-36

The general message of Luke 17: 34-36 is the same as that of Matthew 24: 40-41. Suddenly, as quickly as lightning comes from East to West, an event which is sudden and unexpected will occur. Two men will be on a business trip sleeping in twin beds, and without any warning one will be gone. Two women will be shopping together and suddenly, in the blink of an eye, one cannot be found. Two men will be framing a new house, and one moment they will be nailing a rafter and in the next it will come crashing down because one end will not be supported. The ones who remain will say: *What is going on*? There will be no clue as to what has just happened because everyone left behind will be an unbeliever. Even more striking, in some large cemetery a man will be beside the grave of His wife that had died years before, and suddenly he will be surrounded by empty graves. His best friend is gone, his mother is gone and his wife is gone: It will be an unbelievable experience!

> *But know this, that if the goodman of the house had known in what* **watch** *the thief would come, he would have watched, and would not have suffered his house to be broken up*   Matthew 24:43

The term *watch* does not mean to observe. The context is not one connotating imminency. It is referring to the Roman and Greek method of identifying night hours in the 1st century. The Jews, Greeks and

Romans, each divided the night into military watches instead of hours, The Jews originally used only three such watches: The 1st or beginning of the watches (Lamentations 2:19); the 2nd or middle watch (Judges 7:19); and the 3rd or the morning watch (Exodus 14:24; I Samuel 11:11). These were 4 hours each in duration: 6:00 PM to 10:00 PM; 10:00 PM to 2:00 AM; and from 2:00 AM to 6:00 AM. After the Romans made Israel a vassal state, the number of watches were increased to four. These were each 3 hours in duration, and were described either according to their numerical order....1 to 4 (Matthew 14:25) or by the terms *evening, midnight, cock-crowing* or morning (Mark 13:35).

> [42] Watch therefore: for ye know not what hour your Lord doth come.
> [43] But know this, that if the goodman of the house had known in what watch the thief would come, he would have watched, and would not have suffered his house to be broken up   Matthew 24: 42-43

Christ did *not* say that there would be no signs that precede the rapture of the Saints, nor did He say not to anticipate when the rapture would occur (Feast of Trumpets). He said that each should *watch* for the *hour* at which He might come. The hour of His blessed appearance is certainly different in different parts of the world.

> [44] Therefore be ye also ready: for in such an hour as ye think not the Son of man cometh.
> [45] Who then is a faithful and wise servant, whom his lord hath made ruler over his household, to give them meat in due season?
> Matthew 24: 44-45

The message is always the same: *Be watchful! Be ready!!* Remember the context and setting of Matthew 24. These were His apostles who had little understanding of what Christ was saying. He was answering the questions that were asked by Peter, James, John and Andrew (Mark 13: 3-4) as they left the Temple of Herod. There was probably no comprehensive understanding of what was about to happen to their Lord and Savior. There was no knowledge (as far as we know) concerning the Church age, salvation by Faith, the Book of Revelation and the rapture of all born-again believers more than 2000 years in the future. We are extremely fortunate to have the New Testament, the prophecies of the Old Testament prophets, and the 13 epistles of Paul. Even possessing a complete bible in English was just a dream until the 1st English bible was translated from Latin in 1535 AD and published. It was still not universally available until the first King James Bible was published in 1611 AD.

There will be many who have not read this book or any other book that attempts to explain and investigate the rapture… good Christians who have only casually read the Book of Revelation and never heard of the 7 Feasts of Israel. Please saints…be watchful, be prepared and be conversant on the Book of Revelation. Remember the *Parable of the Wise and Foolish Virgins*. They were all *virgins* and all had *lamps* which at one time were burning brightly. Five were not ready when the Groom came for his bride. They rose to meet the groom, but they did not have any oil in their lamps. The *5 Foolish Virgins* said to the *5 Wise Virgins* who arose to meet the groom, trimmed their torches and lighted their lamps: *Give me some of your oil*; but no one could. No one can give you eternal life but Jesus Christ the Son of God, and no one can give you the oil of eternal light but Jesus Christ who is the light of the world. Who then is the *wise and faithful servant* that Jesus Christ will call to Him when He comes?

For those who have not studied prophecy, it will certainly be true that: *in such an hour as ye think not the Son of man cometh.* Other than a knowledge and understanding of Matthew 24, the Book of Daniel, the Old Testament prophets and the Book of Revelation …. *What does Christ expect of those He has chosen when He suddenly arrives again?* We should have no doubt as to what we should be doing when Christ comes again.

> *Blessed is that servant, whom his lord when he cometh shall find so doing*   Matthew 24: 46

So doing, what? Simply going to church or serving pie at a Christmas bake sale?? Certainly, these are good works, but Christ said: *Pick up your cross and follow me. If you love me, you will do what I have commanded you to do..*

- Be gracious, forgiving and merciful to others.
- Share the riches and wealth that God has given you in this world with those less fortunate
- Forgive those who persecute you
- Do not be haughty, better-than- thou, or exalt things which God has given us
- Do what you can for the poor, sick, needy, abused and lost

But, it's not simply good works that make someone a Christian.

[14] *What doth it profit, my brethren, though a man say he hath faith, and have not works? can faith save him?*
[15] *If a brother or sister be naked, and destitute of daily food,*
[16] *And one of you say unto them, Depart in peace, be ye warmed and filled; notwithstanding ye give them not those things which are needful to the body; what doth it profit?*
[17] *Even so faith, if it hath not works, is dead, being alone.*
[18] *Yea, a man may say, Thou hast faith, and I have works: shew me thy faith without thy works, and I will shew thee my faith by my works.*
[19] *You believe that there is one God; thou doest well: the devils also believe, and tremble.*
[20] *But wilt thou know, O vain man, that faith without works is dead?*
[21] *Was not Abraham our father justified by works, when he had offered Isaac his son upon the altar?*
[22] *Seest thou how faith wrought with his works, and by works was*

faith made perfect?
[23] *And the scripture was fulfilled which saith, Abraham believed God, and it was imputed unto him for righteousness: and he was called the Friend of God.*
[24] *Ye see then how that by works a man is justified, and not by faith only*   James 2: 14-24

Being a follower and disciple of Jesus extends beyond our outward behavior. It includes the condition of our heart. It should be crystal clear that good works never saved anyone, but read the letter which Christ wrote to the Church at Laodicea (Revelation 3: 14-21) and to the Church at Ephesus (Revelation 2: 1-11) with fear and trepidation.

(you say that) *I* (Laodiceans) *am rich, and increased with goods, and have need of nothing; and knowest not that thou art wretched, and miserable, and poor, and blind, and naked*   Revelation 3:17

[4] *Nevertheless I have somewhat against thee, because thou hast left thy first love.*
[5] *Remember therefore from whence thou art fallen, and repent, and do the first works; or else I will come unto thee quickly, and will remove thy candlestick out of his place, except thou repent*
Revelation 2: 4-5

I am persuaded that if a person loves Jesus Christ, that he/she will do as Christ our Lord and Savior commanded us to do. However, I am also persuaded that no one will ever lose his/her salvation due to lack of works. It is not a matter of *having* to serve our Lord and Savior on a daily basis and having the right attitude when we do it…....It is a matter that anyone who is saved by the finished work of Jesus Christ on the Cross of Calvary and is cleansed by the precious blood of Jesus Christ will *want* to serve Him on a daily basis. Should we quit fishing, golfing or hunting? Only if it supersedes your love for Christ and becomes the

#1 thing in your life. All believers will be judged for works at the *Bema Seat Judgment*...Not for salvation but rewards.

> [48] *But and if that evil servant shall say in his heart, My lord delays his coming;*
> [49] *And shall begin to smite his fellow-servants, and to eat and drink with the drunken;*
> [50] *The lord of that servant shall come in a day when he looks not for him, and in an hour that he is not aware of,*
> [51] *And shall cut him asunder, and appoint him his portion with the hypocrites: there shall be weeping and gnashing of teeth.*
> Matthew 24: 48-51

The responsibility and attitude of those who do not watch and be prepared for the 2nd coming of Jesus Christ are summarized in Matthew 24: 48-51. There will be many Christians who will be surprised to learn that the Tribulation period is not 7 years long as most prophecy teachers claim. Satan will not begin his campaign of death, destruction and persecution of all Jews and Christians until he is cast out of the heavenlies by Micheal and his angels. As the signs of the 1st four seals unfold, there will be wars and rumers of wars, famine, death and pestilence on an unprecedented scale. These will intensify until every person on earth will suddenly see a great heavenly conflict. The uninformed Christian will believe: *Just hang on because we (all Christians) will be raptured out before Satan begins his reign of terror over the last 3.5 years.* Since they will be convinced and have been told that the persecution of Satan as the 7 Trumpet judgments are each initiated by 7 angels at the command of God, many will eat, drink and be merry without preparing for the onslaught of Satan, the Antichrist and the False Prophet. Our Lord Jesus Christ will come, but not until 1250 days of the 1260-day tribulation period have elapsed (Phillips, *A New Pre-Wrath Rapture Theory*). By extension, those who ignore the signs which precede the rapture of all born-again believers as the 7th trumpet sounds (Phillips, *The 7 Feasts of Israel*: Phillips; *A New Pre-Wrath Rapture Theory*) will not be ready and Christ: *shall cut him asunder, and appoint him his portion with the hypocrites: there shall be weeping and gnashing of teeth.* How sad it will be for those who are worldly, ambitious, and just *hanging on* until they are raptured out. They believe that the body of Christ will *not* be responsible for saving millions of Jews and millions of unbelievers ……How sad. There will be many who will be deceived by those who teach a Pre-Tribulation Rapture, and those who ignore the words of Christ words in the Olivet Discourse and the details written in the Book of Revelation. It is difficult for anyone to ignore what Christ told His Apostles, and us to watch for and expect when the Great Tribulation begins.

> [9] *Then shall they deliver you up to be afflicted, and shall kill you: and ye shall be hated of all nations for my name's sake.*
> [10] *And then shall many be offended, and shall betray one another, and shall hate one another.*
> [11] *And many false prophets shall rise, and shall deceive many.*
> [12] *And because iniquity shall abound, the love of many shall wax cold.*
> [13] *But he that shall endure unto the end, the same shall be saved.*
> Matthew 24: 9-13

This does not sound like a Pre-Tribulation rapture. *What does Christ expect each of His elect to be doing when He comes again?*

Chapter 6

The Wise and Foolish Virgins

Christ had not yet finished His Olivet Discourse. He uses three parables to explain what the end will be like for those who are not prepared for His 2nd Advent: (1) The *Parable of the Wise and Foolish Virgins* (2) The *Parable of the Fig Tree* and (3) *The Parable of the Talents*. These Parables were spoken by Christ to His Apostles on Mt. Sinai and applied primarily to the Jews. However, salvation was subsequently offered to Jews and Gentiles alike and the message also has application to the Gentiles. The New Covenant was completely hidden from Israel when Christ delivered the Olivet Discourse. The 1st part of the Olivet Discourse was given to answer the following questions for the Jews.

Tell us, when shall these things be? and what shall be the sign of thy coming, and of the end of the world?   Matthew 24:3

The same questions were answered with much more detail for both Jews and Gentiles when John wrote the Book of Revelation. Hence, although the Book of Revelation was not written until around 90 AD - 95 AD, the details revealed by Christ to John in the Book of Revelation must not conflict with the discourse first spoken by Christ on the Mt. of Olives.

The Parables which Jesus spoke in the Olivet Discourse were spoken only to the Jews. In a broader sense, it was spoken as the 70th Week of Daniel began to reach its halfway point and answered a question posed by Daniel over 480 years earlier: *What would be the final fate of his beloved Jews?* (Daniel 9). Christ wanted to assure the Jews…who were God's chosen people…that they would not be forgotten. Within a matter of hours (48 hours or less) Jesus would be crucified on the Cross of

Calvary, and by His sacrificial death all sins of both Jews and Gentiles would be permanently forgiven. Israel and the Jews would be set aside by God during the *Age of Faith and Grace*, after the Jewish spiritual leaders and the Jews corporately rejected His Son Jesus Christ. God would also anoint Saul of Tarsus (Paul) and the Gentiles to evangelize the world, preach the Gospel of salvation by faith and build the Body of Christ until it is completed. The Jews would be *blinded in part* (John 12:40, Romans 11:25) until Satan is cast out of the heavenlies and the Great Tribulation begins. As a corporate body, they would not accept Jesus Christ as their Lord and Savior until the Latter days of the Great Tribulation. When Satan is cast out of the heavenlies by Micheal and his Holy Angels (Revelation 12: 7-8), this will initiate the last 3.5 years of Daniel's 70th Week. During these 3.5 years God will once again be dealing with the Jews as his chosen people, but salvation will be by faith and grace. During this same 3.5 years, Jesus will complete His *Body of Christ,* and *all of Israel will be saved* (Romans 11: 26-27). Christ likened the Kingdom of Heaven to 10 virgins.

> [1] *Then shall the kingdom of heaven be likened unto ten virgins, which took their lamps, and went forth to meet the bridegroom.*
> [2] ***And five of them were wise, and five were foolish.***
> [3] *They that were foolish took their lamps, and took no oil with them:*
> [4] *But the wise took oil in their vessels with their lamps.*
> [5] *While the bridegroom tarried, they all slumbered and slept.*
> [6] *And at midnight there was a cry made, Behold, the bridegroom cometh; go ye out to meet him.*
> [7] *Then all those virgins arose, and trimmed their lamps.*
> [8] *And the foolish said unto the wise, Give us of your oil; for our lamps are gone out.*
> [9] *But the wise answered, saying, Not so; lest there be not enough for us and you: but go ye rather to them that sell, and buy for yourselves.*
> [10] *And while they went to buy, the bridegroom came; and they that were ready went in with him to the marriage: and the door was shut.*

> [11] *Afterward came also the other virgins, saying, Lord, Lord, open to us.*
> [12] *But he answered and said, Verily I say unto you, I know you not.*
> [13] *Watch therefore, for ye know neither the day nor the hour wherein the Son of man cometh*   Matthew 25: 1-13

It is my belief that this parable has been misinterpreted by many fine biblical scholars. It is important to not only notice what Christ *said,* but what He *did not say*. He did not mention in detail the bride or the groom; and He did not mention any wedding guests. The parable is to the Jews only, and it is concerned with being ready and being prepared for the end of the age, which is the last half of Daniel's 70th Week. This parable is usually interpreted as being about the rapture of the Ecclesia and being ready and prepared for Jesus Christ. However, it is my belief that this parable is a prophecy to both Jews and Gentiles, and concerns the necessity of being born-again. The persecution of Satan will be directed to both Jews and Gentiles, and the rapture will include all New Covenant believers. The Wrath of Satan will begin when Satan is cast down.

> [1] *And there appeared a great wonder in heaven; a woman clothed with the sun, and the moon under her feet, and upon her head a crown of twelve stars:*
> [2] *And she being with child cried, travailing in birth, and pained to be delivered.*
> [3] *And there appeared another wonder in heaven; and behold a great red dragon, having seven heads and ten horns, and seven crowns upon his heads.*
> [4] *And his tail drew the third part of the stars of heaven, and did cast them to the earth: and the dragon stood before the woman which was ready to be delivered, for to devour her child as soon as it was born.*
> [5] *And she brought forth a man child, who was to rule all nations with a rod of iron: and her child was caught up unto God, and to his throne*
> Revelation 12: 1-5

Who is this Sun-Clothed Woman who suddenly appears in Revelation 12:1? The woman can be identified by studying a dream that Joseph had in Genesis 37.

The dream of Joseph is only referenced twice in all of the Holy Scriptures: Genesis 37: 9-11 and Revelation 12:1). The Sun Clothed Woman in both Genesis and Revelation is *Israel* (Genesis 37:9). The imagery in Revelation 12:1 recalls the dream that Joseph had concerning the *sun* (Jacob) and the *moon* (Rachel) and the *12 patriarchs* of the nation Israel (12 stars).

The *dragon* in Revelation 12:3 is Satan. As the Great Tribulation approaches, the Sun clothed woman is described as a *woman travailing in childbirth* (Revelation 12:2) and this is additional evidence that the *sun clothed woman* is Israel.

[7] Before she travailed, she brought forth; before her pain came, she was delivered of a man child.
[8] Who hath heard such a thing? who hath seen such things? Shall the earth be made to bring forth in one day? or shall a nation be born at once? for as soon as Zion travailed, she brought forth her children Isaiah 66: 7-8

The Sun-Clothed Woman (Israel) is travailing in child-birth (Revelation 12:2) and about to birth a man-child (Revelation 12:10). *Who is this man-child?* The traditional interpretation is that this Man-child is Jesus Christ, but this cannot be true. *First*, the scene which John saw in Revelation 12 is one which predicts how the *Great Tribulation* will begin. *Second*, if the Man-Child is Jesus Christ His mother was Mary. If so, Jesus would be caught up to heaven at His birth. *Third*, the Sun-clothed Woman is clearly Israel. *Fourth*, If the Man-Child is Christ, this vision would have to refer to the 1st century AD. This would be out of context with all prophetic content of the Book of Revelation. *Fifth*, the Man-Child is caught up alive to the Throne of God, and Christ was crucified as a 33-year-old man. He ascended in the spirit 3 days later. The evidence suggests that we need to look elsewhere.

The woman (Israel) is about to give birth to a Man-Child. The Man-Child is to *rule over all Nations with* a *Rod of Iron*, promised in Revelation 2:27 to all New Covenant believers who are overcomers. (I John 5: 4-5).

And he shall rule them with a rod of iron; as the vessels of a potter shall they be broken to shivers: even as I received of my Father
Revelation 2:27

So: *Who is this Man-child?* This Man-Child is *Israel* because it will be birthed from Israel (the Sun-Clothed woman). This Man-Child is the *Firstfruits* of the Jews who will corporately accept Jesus Christ as their Savior (Revelation 14:4). The Man-Child is *caught up* to God and to His throne (Revelation 12:5). The phrase *caught up* (Matthew 12:5) is the English Translation of the Greek word *Harpazo*, which means to be *snatched away*. It is the same Greek word used by Paul in when he revealed that the saints would be caught up by what we call the *rapture*.

[16] *For the Lord himself shall descend from heaven with a shout, with the voice of the archangel, and with the trump of God: and the dead in Christ shall rise first:*
[17] *Then we which are alive and remain shall be* **caught up** *together with them in the clouds, to meet the Lord in the air: and so shall we ever be with the Lord* I Thessalonians 4:17

This catching-away of the Man-child is a rapture, but it is *not* the rapture revealed by Paul. Note the obvious difference: (1) The Man-Child in Revelation 12 is all Jews (2) The Man-Child is caught up directly to God and His throne, they do not meet Christ in the air. This Man-Child is further described in Revelation 14 and are seen in Matthew 14:1-5 standing on the *heavenly* Mt. Zion with the *Lamb of God*, Jesus Christ.

[1] *And I looked, and, lo, a Lamb stood on the mount Sion, and with him* **an hundred forty and four thousand**, *having his Father's name written in their foreheads.*
[2] *And I heard a voice from heaven, as the voice of many waters, and as the voice of a great thunder: and I heard the voice of harpers harping with their harps:*
[3] *And* **they sung a new song** *before the throne, and before the four beasts, and the elders: and no man could learn that song but the hundred and forty and four thousand, which were redeemed from the earth.*
[4] *These are they which were not defiled with women; for* **they are virgins**. *These are they which follow the Lamb whithersoever he goeth. These were redeemed from among men, being the* **Firstfruits** *unto God and to the Lamb.*
[5] *And in their mouth was found no guile: for they are without fault* **before the throne of God**   Revelation 14: 1-5

This Man-Child numbers 144,000, which is the same number as those sealed by God in Revelation 7: 1-8. These are two different groups but they are all Jews. The 144,000 in Revelation 14 are snatched away to heaven before the throne of God. The 144,000 in Revelation 7: 1-8 are from 12 tribes of Israel, and they are sealed to survive the Wrath of Satan and the Wrath of God (Revelation 15:1, Revelation 16:1) so that they can inherit the 1000-year Millennial Kingdom; procreate, and live there as real humans. (Phillips, *Life after the Great Tribulation*, Zachariah 8). During the Great Tribulation, the 144,000 Jews in Revelation 7 will witness for Jesus Christ along with the two in Revelation 11: 3-4. They are sealed to survive the Wrath of God and inherit the Millennial Kingdom. The two witnesses in Revelation 11:3 are *not* sealed, and they will be martyred by Satan (Revelation 11:7).

The group of Revelation 14 sing a *new song* to God and appear with four beasts and elders which stand before God (Revelation 14:1) on the heavenly Mt. Zion (Revelation 14:3). *What does this mean?* The old song was the Song of Moses (Exodus 15:1) which the Israelites sang to celebrate their delivery from Pharoah and his army at the Red Sea. This is a new song because it is being sung to God as His bride, and to Jesus Christ for redeeming them.

And they overcame him (Satan) *by the blood of the Lamb, and by the word of their testimony*   Revelation 12:11

The Man-child is a group of *Jewish Firstfruits* (Revelation 14: 3-4). The concept of a Firstfruits Harvest originated after the Exodus when Israel began to occupy the Promised Land and became an agricultural nation. As the grain crop (barley and wheat) began to mature, a sheath of barley would be picked by the High Priest, taken to the temple, and on the following morning *waved to the Lord*. The Firstfruit harvest was the best of the new crop, and it was offered to the Lord before any further harvest could take place. No grain could be reaped, sold, or eaten unless God accepted the Firstfruits offering. This was to take place on the Feast of Firstfruits, which was one of the 7 Feasts of Israel (Phillips, *The 7 Feasts of Israel*). Christ satisfied the Feast of Firstfruits when God raised Him from the grave after 3 days and 3 nights. He ascended to heaven and was accepted as the perfect sacrificial lamb for the sins of the world. Christ was the **Firstfruits offering** of all who would be saved under the New Covenant. Christ was the First of the Firstfruits.

But now is Christ risen from the dead, and become the Firstfruits of them that slept   I Corinthians 15: 20

The 144,000 in Revelation 14:4 are called *virgins*, and they are not *defiled* with women *What does this mean?* These are they which were not defiled with the whore of Revelation 17: 1-5, and her spiritual harlots. The kings and inhabitants of the earth were drunk with the wine of her fornication, and they practiced idolatry, which is spiritual fornication. These 144,000 were free from such practices The term *virgin* has nothing to do with celibacy or marriage. It also cannot mean sinless, for: *All have sinned and fallen short of the glory of God.* They are called virgins, but this is not virginity in the physical sense of marital intercourse (Barnes Commentary on Revelation 14).

(a) Whatever may be said anywhere of the purity of virgins, there is no condemnation or commendation of an unmarried man or woman who have not had sexual relationships.

(b) It cannot be supposed that God meant in any way to reflect on the married life as being impure or dishonorable;

(c) The language does not demand such an interpretation.

The *Wise Virgins* will be raptured away and join God in Heaven. The *Foolish Virgins* will have to stay on the earth and go through the Wrath of God. The Wise Virgins were born-again Christians and the Foolish Virgins were not. It is important to note that they were all *virgins*. They all professed to be Christians who were ready to attend the Marriage of the Lamb (raptured); but something was terribly wrong.

Those who are called *wise virgins* have accepted Christ as their Savior, and understand what it means to be called a *Christian*. The Wise Virgins have been born-again and live their life serving Christ. The Foolish Virgins had the appearance of being born-again but they had not fully committed to Jesus Christ.

The Foolish Virgins can be seen in any church on any Sunday. They believe in Jesus Christ, but they are not fully committed. They are not hypocrites, but they have not completely abandoned the call of the world and sold out to Jesus. Jesus Christ said: *You must be born again* (John 3:3, I Peter 1:23), and all who are born again become a completely new creature in Christ. Any other definition of a *virgin* does serious damage to the full council of scripture. We will see that this definition of a virgin is consistent with the fate of the five Foolish Virgins. Christ had previously defined a born-again Christian.

[21] *Not ever one that saith unto me, Lord, Lord, shall enter into the kingdom of heaven; but he that doeth the will of my Father which is in heaven.*
[22] *Many will say to me in that day, Lord, Lord, have we not prophesied in thy name? and in thy name have cast out devils? and in thy name done many wonderful works?*
[23] *And then will I profess unto them, I never knew you: depart from me, ye that work iniquity*   Matthew 7: 21-23

For many are called, but few are chosen   Matthew 22:14

What was the determining factor? It was the *oil* and it was stated in Matthew 25: 3-4.

> [3] They that were foolish took their lamps, and took no oil with them:
> [4] But the wise took oil in their vessels with their lamps
> Matthew 25: 3-4

There is only one obvious difference between the Wise and Foolish Virgins... The Wise virgins had *Oil* for their lamps and the Foolish virgins did not. *What is this oil?* In the 1st century AD, the oil which was not the same as that sold today as a petroleum by-product, but was *olive oil*.

The Greek word translate *lamps* is actually *torches*. The average person made torches out of a tightly wound fibrous material caller *reeds*. These reeds would be twisted into a torch which would contain a central portion called a *wick*. The wick would be soaked in wax made from animal fat called *tallow*. The wick would be immersed in a *reservoir* which contained olive oil. The wax-soaked wick would draw the olive oil to the top of the torch and when lit it would produce *light*. In the Holy Scriptures, *Olive Oil* is often a type of the *Holy Spirit* (Luke 4:18, Acts 10:38, I Samuel 16:13, Isaiah 61:1, I John 2:27). In this parable, the *Oil* is the determining factor as to who will be a part of the Wise Virgins and those who will not.

All 10 Virgins had *lamps*, but only the 5 Wise Virgins had enough Oil for their lamps *How can any Jewish believer in Jesus Christ be sure that they will be in this group?* The answer is in the scriptures and it is very clear. Jesus plainly said:

Jesus answered and said unto him, Verily, verily, I say unto thee: Except a man be born again, he cannot see the kingdom of God   John 3:3

This is clear and emphatic. You **must** be born again. *What does this mean?* Unfortunately, most pastors equate this with confessing your sins and repenting. Certainly, repentance is *part* of being born again, but an altar call to confess your sins and then be saved is nonsense… and not scriptural. Your sins are already forgiven by the blood of Jesus: This was the great work of Jesus Christ on the Cross of Calvary. Salvation is a free gift to all who would accept Jesus Christ as the Son of God; believe that He was dead and buried…resurrected on the 3rd day…and now sits on the Throne of God as the pure, sacrificial Lamb of God who bore the sins of the world. This faith is the choice of every individual. Sin is no longer a barrier to eternal salvation. One only needs to recognize their sinful acts, and then repent of them. *Repent* means to: *Turn around go the other way*. The atoning work of Jesus Christ on the cross took care of the sin issue… *permanently*. He also said:

[5] *……Verily, verily, I say unto thee: Except a man be born of water and of the Spirit, he cannot enter into the kingdom of God.*
[6] *That which is born of the flesh is flesh; and that which is born of the Spirit is spirit.*
Marvel not that I said unto thee: **Ye must be born again**.
John 3: 5-7

When a person is born-again, he/she is convicted of being a sinner and that person dies to sin. Anyone who is born-again is spiritually transformed into a new creature in Jesus Christ. Forgiveness of sins is an accomplished fact under the New Covenant, but when Christ spoke the Olivet Discourse the New Covenant had not been ratified by His sacrificial death and accepted by God as a Firstfruit offering. John preached *repentance* at the river Jordan to prepare the way for the New Covenant. Repentance signifies a profound transformation or conversion experience, when an individual turns away from a life apart from God and accepts Jesus Christ as Lord and Savior. This experience is *marked* with repentance, *sustained* with faith, and is a *commitment* to follow Christ. Water Baptism is a confirmation and seal of this transformation. This is a life-changing experience, and only Christ can know when this happens. When one is Born-again, that person will receive the *Holy Spirit* which is the *seal of redemption*. The same Holy Spirit baptizes us into the body of Christ (Phillips, *Difficult Passages in the Holy Scriptures*), and regenerates the heart when one gives his mind, heart and spirit to Jesus Christ. Paul also developed this idea of being sealed by the Spirit in Ephesians 1.

In whom ye also trusted, after that ye heard the word of truth, the gospel of your salvation: in whom also after that ye believed, ye were sealed with that holy Spirit of promise   Ephesians 1:13

This sealing takes place when one is Born-again The test of genuineness for the Christian is *perseverance* in faith and *holiness* in life.

The 10 virgins represent *all* who thought that they had been redeemed, saved and born-again… but sadly 5 had not. The division of the 10 virgins into two groups of 5 *do not* imply that 50% will be raptured away and half will not. The virgins who were ready were *wise, and* those who were not were *foolish*.

They all had *lamps*, but only the Wise Virgins brought *oil* with them. The foolish virgins did not have the Holy Spirit in them…. they had never been born-again (John 3:3).

> [5] *While the bridegroom tarried, they all slumbered and slept.*
> [6] *And at midnight there was a cry made, Behold, the bridegroom cometh; go ye out to meet him*   Matthew 25: 5-6

Here is a great truth which characterized *all* of the 10 virgins. They knew that the groom was coming, and all had been waiting and watching… but they *all slumbered and slept* when he actually came. The world is sinking deeper and deeper into apostacy and sin, and the *midnight hour* is fast approaching. Timothy warned us that things will not get better as the end nears, but will get much worse.

[1] *This know also, that in the last days perilous times shall come.*
[2] *For men shall be lovers of their own selves, covetous, boasters, proud, blasphemers,* **disobedient to parents**, *unthankful, unholy,*
[3] **Without natural affection**, *trucebreakers, false accusers, incontinent, fierce, despisers of those that are good,*
[4] *Traitors, heady, high minded,* **lovers of pleasures** *more than lovers of God;*
[5] *Having a form of godliness, but denying the power thereof:* **from such turn away**   II Timothy 3: 1-5

There should not be too much made of the term: *And at midnight* the groom came (Matthew 25:8). This is not a prophecy by Christ as to when he would return. It only means that as previously stated He will suddenly appear at an hour least expected, even at a time when one might be asleep. This means that all preparations must be made while awake and watching. The world will be at war, not peace: Many Christians who have a torch but no oil will be caught in some sinful act rather than doing the work of God. It will be in a time of spiritual apostacy and sin, rather than a time of worldwide revival. The field will be full of *tares and wheat*. The fishing net will have *good fish* and *bad fish*. Some will be caught in acts of adultery instead of in prayer.

> **Then all those virgins arose, and trimmed their lamps   Matthew 25:7**

It is important that *all* arose to trim their lamps. The purpose of trimming their lamps was to make sure that they would burn and produce light. After a lamp has been burning and is extinguished, the wick which draws oil from the lamp turns black and hard. It will not light and burn unless the chaff is cut off (trimmed). They *all* thought that they were ready. They were all professing Christians, but 5 were prepared and ready and 5 were not. I am going to present a parable to you from me. I have a 15-year-old dog in my house. He is old, deaf, and blind… but he is prepared for each day. He can successfully negotiate my living room and even go outside for a short distance without running into anything. At one time, he could see and run but not now…. his time is near. Every Christian should be like my little dog. He has run the course but He is ready for His sure and ultimate fate. The light He once knew has taught Him all he needs to know as long as things do not change…and they will not. All tables, chairs and couches are in place and He knows: His midnight hour is fast approaching, and soon if there is a dog heaven, he will see the light again. He has been faithful, lived a good life and is ready to receive his reward. He has loved me unconditionally and has served me well. I hope that I am as prepared as he must be when the time comes.

[5] *But watch thou in all things, endure afflictions, do the work of an evangelist, make full proof of thy ministry.*
[6] *For I am now ready to be offered, and the time of my departure is at hand.*
[7] *I have fought a good fight, I have finished my course, I have kept the faith:*
[8] *Henceforth there is laid up for me a crown of righteousness, which*

the Lord, the righteous judge, shall give me at that day: and not to me only, but unto all them also that love his appearing   II Timothy 4: 5-8

All of the virgins arose and *all* trimmed their lamps (Matthew 25:7). They all had lamps which were previously burning, but something was wrong. The Foolish Virgins said: *Give us of your oil; for our lamps are gone out* (Matthew 25:8). However, this is *not* what Christ said. He said: *They that were foolish took their lamps, and took no oil with them* (Matthew 25:3). The lamp of light which was once burning had gone out, but even if trimmed it would not burn without oil (Regeneration by the Holy Spirit).

The 5 who had no oil pleaded with the other 5 who had trimmed and lighted their lamps: *Give us some of your oil*. Here is a great spiritual truth. Only God can give a person the Holy Spirit. No one can give you a personal and intimate relationship with God, and no one can make your light shine.

> And the foolish said unto the wise: Give us of your oil; for our lamps are gone out   Matthew 25:8

Just like the Foolish Virgins, there are many people in churches today who THINK they are saved, but have never committed their lives to Christ……. have never been born again……. and are not saved. They go to church all the time. They know the Bible. They think they have the oil of the Holy Spirit. But in reality, they do not. This is not just a casual observation. Christ said: YOU MUST BE BORN AGAIN, and when you are born again your salvation is sealed and guaranteed by the Holy Spirit. This cannot be over-emphasized, over-looked or over-preached. They are practicing religion without any real relationship with Christ. The wick (persons) will draw the *oil* (Holy Spirit) that sustains the righteous, but it must be replaced daily.

Matthew 25:9 is the response which the 5 Wise Virgins gave the 5 Foolish Versions, and it is difficult to interpret.

> But the wise answered, saying: Not so, lest here be not enough for us and you: but go ye rather to them that sell, and buy for yourselves
> Matthew 25:9

It is a fact that no one can **buy** the Holy Spirit…It is a gift from God at the request of Jesus Christ.

[14]..I will pray the Father, and he shall give you another Comforter, that he may abide with you forever;
[17] Even the Spirit of truth; whom the world cannot receive, because it does not see him neither know him: but ye know him; for he dwelleth with you, and shall be in you.
[18] I will not leave you comfortless: I will come to you.
*[26] But the Comforter, which is the **Holy Ghost**, whom the Father will send in my name, **he shall teach you all things, and bring all things to your remembrance**, whatsoever I have said unto you*
John 14: 14, 17-18, 26

What does Matthew 25:9 mean? After studying hundreds of commentaries on Matthew 25, I cannot find one good explanation. Some say that those who sell are preachers, but I categorically reject this interpretation. NO ONE can sell salvation or the Holy Spirit…...it cannot be bought. Jesus Christ paid the full price for our sins on the Cross of Calvary. In Revelation 3:18 Christ counseled the members of the Church at Laodicea:

*I counsel thee to **buy** of me gold tried in the fire, that thou mayest be rich; and white raiment, that thou mayest be clothed, and that the shame of thy nakedness does not appear; and anoint thine eyes with eye salve, that thou may see.*   Revelation 3:18

How can you buy salvation? Isaiah the prophet told us that we can buy without money!

*...every one that thirsts, come ye to the waters, and he that hath no money; come ye, buy, and eat; yea, come, buy wine and milk **without money and without price**.* Isaiah 55:1

The oil of the Holy Spirit will lead you in all things and will allow your light to *shine*. We were made to shine with the glory of Jesus Christ. God created each of us to let our light shine both in the day and in the night. There is so much darkness surrounding us and there is so much darkness in the world. You are the *light of the world* and once born-again you will *never* run out of oil.

[13] *Ye are the salt of the earth: but if the salt has lost his savor, wherewith shall it be salted? it is thenceforth good for nothing, but to be cast out, and to be trodden under foot of men.*
[14] *Ye are the light of the world. A city that is set on a hill cannot be hid.*
[15] *Neither do men light a candle, and put it under a bushel, but on a candlestick; and it giveth light unto all that are in the house.*
[16] *Let your light so shine before men, that they may see your good works, and glorify your Father which is in heaven*
Matthew 5: 13-16

Christ was using the word *buy* in Matthew 25:9 to mean that there is only one way to obtain eternal life, and that is by faith in Jesus Christ. Salvation can only be *bought* by the *blood of Jesus Christ*, and He is the only one who could ever pay the price.

[18] *Forasmuch as ye know that **ye were not redeemed with corruptible things, as silver and gold**, from your vain conversation received by tradition from your fathers;*
[19] ***But with the precious blood of Christ**, as of a lamb without blemish*

*and without spot. Jesus gave His life for us, **purchasing our salvation by shedding His blood on the cross**.*   I Peter 1: 18-19

We are now free from the curse of sin, but that freedom does not mean that we can do what every non-believer does in a sinful world.

[13] For if ye live after the flesh, ye shall die: but if ye through the Spirit do mortify the deeds of the body, ye shall live.
[14] For as many as are led by the Spirit of God, they are the sons of God.   Romans 8: 13-14

> And while they went to buy, the bridegroom came; and they that were ready went in with him to the marriage: and the door was shut
> Matthew 25:10

The carnal man cannot communicate with God and cannot understand anything about God because he/she does not have the Holy Spirit. This parable teaches only one distinction between the Wise and the Foolish virgins. It rewards and recognizes five as wise because they bring oil, and it excludes five as foolish for failing to be prepared. Otherwise, all the virgins act the same. They arrive on time. They all wait. They all tire and they all fall asleep. Awakened, they all start to trim their lamps. But when the bridegroom arrives, the foolish virgins discover that their lamps will not light because they have no oil. The five wise virgins, asserting they have only enough oil for themselves, will not share. So, the foolish five go to find and obtain oil, finding the door to the wedding shut upon their return.

> [11] Afterward came also the other virgins, saying, Lord, Lord, open to us.
> [12] But he answered and said, Verily I say unto you, I know you not
> Matthew 25: 11-12

The Foolish Virgins had not fully committed their heart, mind, and lives to Jesus Christ and received the Holy Spirit when Born-again. The fact that Jesus said *I know you not*, shows that in fact they were never saved. *He literally never knew them*. In outward appearance, the Foolish virgins could not be distinguished from the Wise Virgins. The Foolish Virgins had never totally committed to Jesus Christ, never been saved, and never received the Spirit of Promise… the Holy Spirit.

In any case, all 5 Foolish Virgins did as they were told and went to find *oil*. It is apparent that they sought Jesus Christ, they repented, and they thought that they were saved because they returned and said: *Lord, Lord open the door*. The door was *shut* (Matthew 25:10, and the 5 foolish virgins heard those terrible words: *I know you not.* We are reminded of what Christ previously said in Matthew 22:14: *For many are called, but few are chosen*. The foolish virgins were like the stony ground in the *Parable of the Sower*:

[5] *Some fell upon stony places, where they had not much earth: and forthwith they sprung up, because they had no deepness of earth:*
[6] *And when the sun was up, they were scorched; and because they had no root, they withered away* Matthew 13: 5-6

The Foolish Virgins had heard the message of salvation: They committed to knowing Jesus Christ: They were in church every Sunday… but they were never born-again. Those who had accepted Jesus Christ as their Lord and Savior, were born-again and received the Holy Spirit were prepared and ready. They had fully committed to Christ and they found the door *open*. The *Wise Virgins* had heard the commands of God and went through the door with their Lord and Savior.

Behold, I stand at the door, and knock: if any man hears my voice, and open the door, I will come in to him, and will sup with him, and he with me Revelation 3:20

Now a great spiritual truth must be understood. Just because these foolish virgins have missed the *rapture* does not mean that they cannot be saved. Examine the parable carefully. Matthew 25:10 said that the foolish virgins went to buy oil. After a time, they came again with the oil that they did not have…...but it was too late: *the door was shut.*

These Foolish Virgins had missed the rapture, but they sought Jesus Christ and the door to salvation. They went and found the *oil*, but when they returned it was too late to join the *Wise Virgins*. This does not mean they can never be saved. The rapture of all Born-again believers will occur before the Church Age is over. There will be time for the Foolish Virgins to witness as born-again Christians and serve Him with the constant threat of martyrdom hanging over them. During the Great Tribulation there will be many Jews and Gentiles which will turn to Jesus Christ as their Lord and Savior. Those who will be caught up to Christ at the *Last Trump* may have missed the rapture, but they may not not miss the main harvest.

*[25] For I would not, brethren, that ye should be ignorant of this mystery, lest ye should be wise in your own conceits; that blindness in part is happened to Israel, until the fulness of the Gentiles be come in. [26] And so **all Israel shall be saved**: as it is written, There shall come out of Sion the Deliverer, and shall turn away ungodliness from Jacob: [27] For this is my covenant unto them, when I shall take away their* sins Romans 11: 25-27

One of the purposes of the Great Tribulation is to restore the Jews into a covenant relationship with God. During the Wrath of God (7 Bowl Judgments): *all of Israel will be saved.* Be careful to notice that once the Age of grace comes to a close, if anyone does not accept Jesus Christ as their Lord and savior, that person will be cast into the *Lake of Burning Fire* (Revelation 19:20). Those who accept Christ while they are still alive… even at the last hour as the thief on the cross did…will be saved. There will be different levels of reward and service in the Kingdom to come. Everyone will be rewarded according to how they have lived and followed Christ in this life. That is a fundamental truth throughout the entire New Testament.

> Watch therefore, for ye know neither the day nor the hour wherein the Son of man cometh   Matthew 25:13

Matthew 25:13 ends the *Parable of the Wise and Foolish Virgins*. This parable is one of the most revealing in the New Testament.

...And they sang a New Song

Chapter 7
The Parable of the Talents

The *Parable of the Talents* is also part of the Olivet discourse. This is part of what we call the *Kingdom Parables*. The Parable of the *Wise and Foolish Virgins* concern those will be raptured out of the Great tribulation (Matthew 24:22) to be spared from the Wrath of God. The Parable of the Talents is concerned with *what* the Lord should find us doing when He returns. The context of the Parable of the Talents is the Rapture of the saints (Jews and Gentiles) when Christ will gather *all* true believers to him at the main harvest.

> [14] *For the kingdom of heaven is as a man travelling into a far country, who called his own servants, and delivered unto them his goods.*
> [15] *And unto one he gave five talents, to another two, and to another one; to every man according to his several ability; and straightway took his journey.*
> [16] *Then he that had received the five talents went and traded with the same, and made them other five talents.*
> [17] *And likewise he that had received two, he also gained other two.*
> [18] *But he that had received one went and dug in the earth, and hid his lord's money.*
> [19] *After a long time the lord of those servants comes, and reckons with them.*
> [20] *And so he that had received five talents came and brought other five talents, saying, Lord, thou delivered unto me five talents: behold, I have gained beside them five talents more.*
> [21] *His lord said unto him, Well done, thou good and faithful servant: thou hast been faithful over a few things, I will make thee ruler over*

> *enter thou into the joy of thy lord.*
> *[22] He also that had received two talents came and said, Lord, thou delivered unto me two talents: behold, I have gained two other talents beside them.*
> *[23] His lord said unto him, Well done, good and faithful servant; thou hast been faithful over a few things, I will make thee ruler over many things: enter thou into the joy of thy lord.*
> *[24] Then he which had received the one talent came and said, Lord, I knew thee that thou art an hard man, reaping where thou hast not sown, and gathering where thou hast not strawed:*
> *[25] And I was afraid, and went and hid thy talent in the earth: lo, there thou hast that is thine.*
> *[26] His lord answered and said unto him, Thou wicked and slothful servant, thou knew that I reap where I sowed not, and gather where I have not strawed:*
> *[27] Thou ought therefore to have put my money to the exchangers, and then at my coming I should have received mine own with usury.*
> *[28] Take therefore the talent from him, and give it unto him which hath ten talents.*
> *[29] For unto every one that hath shall be given, and he shall have abundance: but from him that hath not shall be taken away even that which he hath.*
> *[30] And cast ye the unprofitable servant into outer darkness: there shall be weeping and gnashing of teeth*   Matthew 25: 14-30

The parable of the Talents is comparable to the Parable of the Pounds (Luke 19: 11-27), which was spoken by Christ to His disciples as He approached Jerusalem for the last time. The Parable of the Talents is not about salvation, but about *rewards* for good works. Notice before we discuss this parable that there are four men who play important roles: *A man of great wealth* (Matthew 25:14) who travels to a far country for a long time, and *three servants* who were given unequal parts of his great wealth to invest wisely while the man was gone. The 1st servant was given *5 pieces* of a great sum of money called a *talent*. The 2nd was given *2 pieces,* and the 3rd was given only *1 piece*. One talent was worth 6000 *Denars*, and a Denar was the standard rate of pay for one day's work of a common laborer. It contained about 38 kilograms of silver. In today's market (2023) a kilo of silver is worth about $800, so a talent would be worth over $30,400. In Jesus' time, one Denar was the average daily pay for a common worker, or about $5.00 a day (Matthew 20: 1-16).

A Rare Denar Coin

Every Christian will be judged and rewarded for their good works. Good works will be *rewarded*, and bad works will be cast aside and *burned like wood, hay and stubble.*

[13] *Every man's work shall be made manifest: for the day shall declare it, because it shall be revealed by fire; and the fire shall try every man's work of what sort it is.*
[14] *If any man's work abide which he hath built thereupon, he shall receive a reward.*
[15] *If any man's work shall be burned, he shall suffer loss: but he himself shall be saved; yet so as by fire*   I Corinthians 3: 11-15

Christians will be judged for rewards at the *Bema Seat Judgment* which will take place after the *Battle of Armageddon* ends the church age.

Scripture makes it quite clear that salvation and eternal life in Jesus Christ does not depend upon anything but *faith*. When a Christian has faith and is Born-again they receive the Holy Spirit, and their name cannot be erased from the *Book of Life*.

> ***Authors Comment***: There is a book which is kept by God called the Book of Life. If anyone experiences a transformation to a born-again believer and becomes a new creature in Christ, he/she receives the Holy Spirit as a guarantee of the promises to all true believers. There is an ongoing debate which is concerned with the following question: *Can a person's name be removed (erased)*

from the Book of Life? The verse most often quoted is Revelation 22:19.

And if any man shall take away from the words of the book of this prophecy, God shall take away his part out of the Book of Life, and out of the holy city, and from the things which are written in this book   Revelation 22:19

Contrast Revelation 22:19 with Revelation 3:5 and I John 5: 4-5.

The following verse has been misinterpreted so many times that it is hard to discover the truth in the biblical literature.

And all that dwell upon the earth shall worship him (The Antichrist), *whose names are not written in the Book of Life of the Lamb slain **from the foundation of the world***
Revelation 13:8

From these verses it seems evident that (1) There is a *Book of Life* (2) It is kept by God (3) It was written before the foundation of the world (4) Before birth, all of their names are written in the Book of Life (5) The Lambs Book of Life is identical to the Book of Life. The controversy is whether a born-again Christian can or cannot cannot have his/her name erased from the Book of Life

The controversy can be resolved by realizing that before the foundation of the world there was a Book of Life written in which the names of every person or child who would be born were written. Each person has the individual choice of how to live and die. *A true Christian is born twice but dies once.... all unbelievers are born once but die twice.*

[14] *And death and hell were cast into the lake of fire. This is the second death.*
[15] *And whosoever was not found written in the book of life was cast into the lake of fire*   Revelation 20: 14-15

All can believe in Christ by faith and receive the free gift of forgiveness of sins and eternal life. …. Sadly, many do not. Those who die an unbeliever will have their name erased from the Book of Life. Those who are true believers will never have their name erased. Incidentally, this solves the mystery of what will happen to infant children who die before the age of reason.

The parable of the talents concerns a man who was very wealthy, and He gave to every servant according to his own ability. He then left and went to *a far country*, expecting each to invest and grow his resources.

> [14] *For the kingdom of heaven is as a man travelling into a far country, who called his own servants, and delivered unto them his goods.*
> [15] *And unto one he gave five talents, to another two, and to another one; to every man according to his ability, and straightway he took his journey.* Matthew 25: 14-15

The landowner calls three of his servants to him and leaves them in charge of his money. To the 1st he leaves 5 talents, to the 2nd he gives two, and to the 3rd he leaves only one. Notice that Christ did not distribute his wealth evenly to his 3 servants. He distributed his 8 talents according to their *ability* (Matthew 25:15). The man did not require a set amount of return on his talents. He has placed his trust in them and expects them to do what they can based upon what he had given them with his resources. The man left immediately, and he was gone a *long time* (Revelation 25:19).

> [16] *Then he that had received the five talents went and traded with the same, and made them other five talents.*
> [17] *And likewise he that had received two, he also gained other two.*
> [18] *But he that had received one went and dug in the earth, and hid his lord's money* Revelation 25: 16-18

> **[19]** *After a long time the lord of those servants cometh, and he reckoned with them.*
> **[20]** *And so he that had received five talents came and brought other five talents, saying, Lord, thou delivered unto me five talents: behold, I have gained beside them five talents more.*
> **[21]** *His lord said unto him, Well done, thou good and faithful servant: thou hast been faithful over a few things, I will make thee ruler over many things: enter thou into the joy of thy lord.*
> **[22]** *He also that had received two talents came and said, Lord, thou delivered unto me two talents: behold, I have gained two other talents beside them.*
> **[23]** *His lord said unto him, Well done, good and faithful servant; thou hast been faithful over a few things, I will make thee ruler over many things: enter thou into the joy of thy lord.* Matthew 25: 19-23

The 1st inquiry is to the one who was given 5 talents. The joyful servant reported that He had wisely invested the 5 talents he was given, and made 5 more. The landowner is pleased and tells him: *Well done, thou good and faithful servant: thou hast been faithful over a few things, I will make thee ruler over many things.*

The master next turns to the servant that he had given 2 talents. The joyful servant reported that He had wisely invested the 2 talents he was given, and he had also made 2 more! The lord is equally pleased with the servant who had made two talents, and he had equal praise for that faithful servant. *Well done, good and faithful servant*. Note that the lord awarded both servants equally. *Because you have been faithful over a few things, I will make you ruler over many things.* This is exactly what was promised to the faithful apostles of Jesus Christ (Matthew 19:28, Luke 22: 28-30). The 1st had invested his money wisely and doubled what had been given to him. The 2nd likewise parlayed the two talents into two more ……both had a 100% return.

Finally, the master turned to the servant that he had given only 1 talent. Before the master could say anything, the servant immediately started to defend himself. He turned to the lord and said:

> [24] ... *Lord, I knew thee that thou art a hard man, reaping where thou hast not sown, and gathering where thou hast not strawed:*
> [25] *And I was afraid, and went and hid thy talent in the earth: lo, there thou hast that is* thine   Matthew 25: 24-25

This man chooses to conceive of his lord as harsh and unreasonable, who asks his servants to perform above their ability and makes no allowance for imperfect service (This is categorically untrue): The lord in his wisdom had allocated his wealth to his servants: *every man according to his several abilities* (Matthew 25:15). This servant was truly unproductive: He advanced neither his master's interests nor his own. The attitude and response of the servant condemned himself*: I knew thou wast one whom it was impossible to serve, one whom nothing would please: exacting what was impracticable, and dissatisfied with what was unattainable.*

Often, the one that has the least gifts is criticized the most. Most Christians do not understand the Holy Spirit and reject the gifts that are bestowed upon them, rejecting all but one or two. When a person exercises only one gift, failure to do just one thing asked of him/her is very noticeable. However, the owner was not so easily fooled with such outrageous and undeserved excuses. This man was also a *hypocrite,* because he calls him *Lord*: he pretended to serve him but did not. If he had, he would have had a true affection for him, faith in him, and would have obeyed his commands. He knew better than to call him a hard, severe, austere man, impossible to please, cruel and uncompassionate. The owner had given him a great deal of money with no strings attached. The owner saw right through all of his excuses and turned his own wicked and slothful thoughts against him: ***You say you knew*** that I reap where I sowed not, and gather where I have not strawed. If you knew that, why did you do nothing? **You knew!** Out of the servant's own mouth He judges him. He repeats his own words which condemn him without accusation.

> [26] *His lord answered and said unto him: Thou wicked and slothful servant, you knew that I reap where I sowed not, and gather where I have not strawed:*
> [27] *You ought therefore to have put my money to the exchangers, and then at my coming I should have received mine own with usury.*
> Matthew 25: 26-27

While the other two faithful servants enter into the Joy of the Lord, the 3rd is banished into *outer darkness.* The punishment might seem harsh. The servant did not lose any money and returned all that he had been given. His punishment was not for sacrilege or rebellion against the laws of God; but he was cast aside for neglect, idleness and dereliction

> [28] *Take therefore the talent from him, and give it unto him which hath ten talents.*
> [29] *For unto every one that hath shall be given, and he shall have abundance: but from him that hath not shall be taken away even that which he hath.*
> [30] *And cast ye the unprofitable servant into outer darkness: there shall be weeping and gnashing of teeth*   Matthew 25: 28-30

of duty. This man was lazy and did want to risk anything at all. This is a very fearful thought. Men endeavor to screen themselves from blame by minimizing their talents, ability, and opportunities: This parable unveils the fallacy of this pretense. The owner gave to each man *according to his ability.* Regardless of what God chooses for us to do, each individual has responsibilities. Spiritual indolence is as serious a sin as active wickedness, and meets with similar punishment (Matthew 25:30). The punitive action against this person is almost too hard to comprehend. It should be recognized by now that the lord in this parable is *Jesus Christ*. His servants are those Christians that He left to spread the Gospel message while He goes on a *long journey*. Note that this parable is for

all Jews and Gentiles that are forming the Body of Christ, but Jesus is speaking to only Jews outside of Jerusalem.

The owner is quick to pass judgment on the unprofitable servant: (1) He takes the one talent and gives it to the servant who had ten (2) He casts the unproductive servant *into outer darkness* where *there shall be weeping and gnashing of teeth.* It is a fact of life that some people are more qualified, more eloquent of speech, and more physically able than others to work tirelessly for the Lord using multiple gifts. Our loving and omniscient Father knows this and by His grace and wisdom, He will give each appropriate gifts and responsibility consistent with his abilities. God will not ask His chosen people to do anything that that person cannot do. His judgment upon the slothful and lazy servant teaches that nonresponse is not acceptable. When one is called to the Christian faith, God expects him/her to serve Him and follow His commands. The following is an answer to the question: *What does God expect me to do?*

The 1st thing God wants us to do is to believe that Jesus Christ is His only Son: The 2nd thing is to believe that by His sacrificial death on the Cross of Calvary all our sins are forgiven: The 3rd is to then accept His free gift of salvation by *faith.* We are hopeless in our sins, and cannot be good enough to *overcome* on our own. That is why Jesus came into the world to take the punishment we deserve (II Corinthians 5:21). When we put our faith in Christ's death and resurrection, we can fulfill our purpose by knowing and glorifying God (Romans 6: 1–6). Jesus will sanctify us by the Holy Spirit and we will become more like Him as we conform to His image (Romans 8:29). So the answer to the question *what does God want me to do?* is to first receive His Son, Jesus Christ, as our Lord and Savior; be born-again and begin a new life in Jesus Christ; and then work for the kingdom as Christ and the Holy spirit calls us.

After we are saved, God wants us to *grow in the grace and knowledge of our Lord and Savior Jesus Christ* (2 Peter 3:18). When the Holy

Spirit baptizes us and places into the Body of Christ (Romans 8:15), we become a *new creature in Christ* that affects every aspect of our lives. Rather than making decisions to please ourselves, we make decisions that will please the Lord (I Corinthians 10:31). Those decisions will be *reflected* by our actions, *accomplished* through the power of the Holy Spirit, and *approved* by God (Galatians 5:16, 25).

Acting as Jesus Christ would in all circumstances requires that we love others unconditionally as Christ loved us. To follow after Christ, we must obey His commands and live by faith, because: *without faith it is impossible to please God* (Hebrews 11: 5-6). We should always treat other people as we would have them treat us (Matthew 7:12)....*Do unto others as we would have them do unto us*.

To do what God wants us to do, we *must forgive* those who sin against us (Matthew 18:23–35). We should rejoice when we forgive others, remembering how God sent His only begotten Son to forgive us (Luke 6: 35–36).

When a person is born again and becomes part of the body of Christ, God does not become merely a part of our lives, He **IS** our life (Galatians 2:20). We must daily deny ourselves, reject the ways of an evil world and take up our cross to follow Him (Luke 9:23). Only when we repent of our sins (I John 1:9) and free our lives from idolatry, worldliness, and sinful acts (I John 5:21) can we walk humbly with God. God wants us to impact our world with the gospel message. Just before He ascended back into heaven, Jesus answered the question *what does God want me to do?*

[19] *Go ye therefore, and teach all nations, baptizing them in the name of the Father, and of the Son, and of the Holy Ghost:*
[20] *Teaching them to observe all things whatsoever I have commanded you: and, lo, I am with you always, even unto the end of the world. Amen.*   Matthew 28: 19–20

This has been called the *Great Commission* and it has been misunderstood by many well-meaning Christians. It does not mean that if anyone hopes to obtain eternal life in Jesus Christ, that when anyone fully commits to being a born-again Christian that one should leave his/her family, friends and daily responsibilities to teach all nations or become a full-time evangelist. This is a wonderful calling, but it is not meant for every Christian. There is work to be done in every city, in every town, in every business and in every neighborhood. Abortion, drugs, apostate religious practices and immoral behavior are everywhere. There is work to be done in foreign fields, but there is also work to be done in ordinary, everyday life. Use all of the resources, time and wealth that God has given you right where you are and God will reward you:

This reaction is what might be expected. He rewards those who work and serve Him, and rejects those who will not serve him. There is one other thing that can be learned from this parable.

He that is faithful in that which is least is faithful also in much: and he that is unjust in the least is unjust also in much   Luke 16:10

The main lesson to be learned from this parable is that the more one grows in Christ, more will be given. Christ will ask that person to take on more responsibility. However, it should be comforting to know that Christ will never give anyone anything to do that is beyond their capabilities.

> And unto one he gave five talents, to another two, and to another one; to every man according to his several abilities: and straightway took his journey   Matthew 25:15

For whosoever hath, to him shall be given, and he shall have more abundance: but whosoever hath not, from him shall be taken away even that he hath   Matthew 13:12

For unto whomsoever much is given, of him shall be much required: and to whom men have committed much, of him they will ask the more.
Luke 12: 48

Many biblical scholars have completely missed the meaning and teaching of this parable. They view this parable as dealing with how one should manage the money that God has given them, and interpret the parable as one of stewardship, even applying it to tithing. An element of the *Parable of the Talents* which is usually ignored is the ultimate fate of the 3rd servant.

> [29] *For unto every one that hath shall be given, and he shall have abundance: but from him that hath not shall be taken away even that which he hath.*
> [30] *And cast ye the unprofitable servant into outer darkness: there shall be weeping and gnashing of teeth*   Matthew 25: 29-30

In should be understood that the parable makes a distinction between those servants who joyfully and resolutely made a 100 % profit on the investment which the owner placed in their care, and the one who only returned what he was given and made no effort whatsoever to serve his master. He was no good to his lord nor to himself. The one servant who was thoughtless and lazy was dealt with severely. He was removed from the prescence of the owner and cast into outer darkness where *there will be weeping and gnashing of teeth*. This can only represent the *lake of burning fire* (Revelation 20: 12-15), where all unbelievers will spend eternity. It is clear that the two men who doubled what the master had given them, and served him with gladness and resolution, represented saved people… and the one who simply buried what was given to him in the ground was unsaved. He had no intention of using what he had been given, and he even believed that his master was a hard and unforgiving man. His lord called him slothful and lazy, and even asked him: *Why didn't you at least put my money in the bank and let it accrue interest*

(Matthew 25:27). Matthew 25: 24-25 shows that the man with only one talent had no love or respect for his master, no intention to work for him and would not obey his simple command. *This is not a description of a born-again Christian.*

In the sight of God, the characteristics which God seek is *commitment* and *faithfulness*. It is important to realize that how we serve God and what we do with what He has given us in this life will come under judgment when Christ returns again; some for rewards (The Bema Seat Judgment) and some for eternal damnation. The prophet Daniel recognized this truth in the Old Testament.

[2] *And many of them that sleep in the dust of the earth shall awake, some to everlasting life, and some to shame and everlasting contempt.* [3] *And they that be wise shall shine as the brightness of the firmament; and they that turn many to righteousness as the stars for ever and ever* Daniel 12: 2-3

In the *Parable of the Talents*, notice how the faithful servants were rewarded.

> *Well done, good and faithful servant; thou hast been faithful over a few things, I will make thee ruler over many things: enter thou into the joy of thy Lord*   Matthew 25:21

The reward for service and faithfulness will be given to both Jews and Gentiles alike (Galatians 3: 28-29). Jesus will return to rule and reign upon this earth for 1000-years during the Millennial Kingdom. Faithful, born-again Christians will rule and reign with Him (Revelation 2: 26-27, 5:10, 20:4, 7: 14-17, II Timothy 2:12, Isaiah 1:36, Isaiah 32:1). The 11 apostles will sit with Him on thrones (Matthew 19:28). Every born-again Christian will be judged and rewarded for their good works (Bema Seat Judgment), and will serve in a capacity proportional to their faithfulness and service. (Hebrews 9:27).

The Parable of the Talents teaches that there are *gifts* given to every Christian who asks. Some are more capable than others in managing and manifesting the gifts of the Holy spirit. Some will not seek or even understand the work of the Holy Spirit. Jesus Christ made this perfectly clear in Matthew 12.

[31] Wherefore I say unto you, All manner of sin and blasphemy shall be forgiven unto men: but the blasphemy against the Holy Ghost shall not be forgiven unto men.
[32] And whosoever speaks a word against the Son of man, it shall be forgiven him: but **whosoever speaks against the Holy Ghost, it shall not be forgiven him***, neither in this world, neither in the world to come.*
[33] Either make the tree good, and his fruit good; or else make the tree corrupt, and his fruit corrupt: for **the tree is known by his fruit**
Matthew 12: 31-33

These principles of Christian Faith are what Christ was teaching in the Parable of the Talents. One man was given ten gifts, the 2nd was given five, and the 3rd only one… each man according to his *ability* (Matthew 25:15). The one who was given only one gift was not damned because he could only manage a single gift, but he was condemned because he did not even try to exercise the one gift he was given. He *buried* his *talent* and did not even try to follow after Jesus Christ. He was worse than one who tries and fails, because he never tried at all. This is one thing which must grieve the Holy Spirit. The Holy Spirit is sent by God at the request of Jesus Christ to dwell in every true believer, and what the servant did with his single *talent* was an abomination to God and the Holy Spirit because he did not even try. Mark the words of Jesus Christ carefully: *All manner of sin and blasphemy shall be forgiven unto men: but the blasphemy against the Holy Ghost shall not be forgiven unto men.*

He who has an ear to hear… Let him hear and understand

Chapter 8
Judgment of the Nations (Judgment of the Sheep and Goats)

The Judgment of the Sheep and Goats (Judgment of the Nations) is the last thing that Jesus Christ will tell His apostles about His 2nd advent in the Olivet Discourse. This is sometimes called a *parable*, but it is not. It describes a judgment and separation of real people exactly the way that it was revealed by Christ. This *judgment* has no apparent parallel in any other gospel account. It is actually a prophecy of a judgment which will take place *after* the Church age is over. Note what Jesus Christ said in Matthew 25:31 concerning when He would judge the nations.

> *When the **Son of man shall come in his glory**, and all the holy angels with him, **then shall he sit upon the throne of his glory**.*
> Matthew 25: 31

The context and proper placement of the *Judgment of the Nations* is when *Christ will set upon His Throne of Glory* (Micah 4: 1-8).

During the Millennial Kingdom, Christ will rule and reign from His Holy Temple which will be on a high plateau outside of Jerusalem (Phillips, *Life after the Great Tribulation*). King David will be resurrected and sit upon his throne, ruling over 12 tribes of Israel (II Samuel 7: 12-16, Isaiah 9: 6-7). The Holy angels will accompany Jesus Christ when He comes to fight the Battle of Armageddon (Revelation 19:14). After Christ defeats

Satan and his army of demons and unbelievers, The Judgment of the Sheep and Goats will probably take place either immediately before or in the initial days of the Millennial Kingdom.

It is obvious from its very beginning that it passes beyond the realm of a parable into that of divine reality (Elliot commentaries).

The description of this Judgment is given in Matthew 25: 31-46. It is lengthy but should be read and carefully studied before further discussion.

> [31] When the Son of man shall come in his glory, and all the holy angels with him, then shall he sit upon the throne of his glory:
>
> [32] And before him shall be gathered all nations: and he shall separate them one from another, as a shepherd divides his sheep from the goats:
>
> [33] And he shall set the sheep on his right hand, but the goats on the left.
>
> [34] Then shall the King say unto them on his right hand, Come, ye blessed of my Father, inherit the kingdom prepared for you from the foundation of the world:
>
> [35] For I was an hungry, and ye gave me meat: I was thirsty, and ye gave me drink: I was a stranger, and ye took me in:
>
> [36] Naked, and ye clothed me: I was sick, and ye visited me: I was in prison, and ye came unto me.
>
> [37] Then shall the righteous answer him, saying, Lord, when saw we thee an hungry, and fed thee? or thirsty, and gave thee drink?
>
> [38] When saw we thee a stranger, and took thee in? or naked, and clothed thee?
>
> [39] Or when saw we thee sick, or in prison, and came unto thee?
>
> [40] And the King shall answer and say unto them, Verily I say unto you, Inasmuch as ye have done it unto one of the least of these my brethren, ye have done it unto me.

> [41] Then shall he say also unto them on the left hand, Depart from me, ye cursed, into everlasting fire, prepared for the devil and his angels:
>
> [42] For I was an hungry, and ye gave me no meat: I was thirsty, and ye gave me no drink:
>
> [43] I was a stranger, and ye took me not in: naked, and ye clothed me not: sick, and in prison, and ye visited me not.
>
> [44] Then shall they also answer him, saying, Lord, when saw we thee an hungry, or athirst, or a stranger, or naked, or sick, or in prison, and did not minister unto thee?
>
> [45] Then shall he answer them, saying, Verily I say unto you, Inasmuch as ye did it not to one of the least of these, ye did it not to me.
>
> [46] And these shall go away into everlasting punishment: but the righteous into life eternal   Matthew 25: 31-46

The portrait of Christ in this passage is as judge and executioner. All the nations of the world have gathered before him and are subject to His majesty. This imagery recalls Jude 1: 14-15 where Jesus Christ will sit in judgment surrounded by a host of angels.

Christ had already revealed a description of who he will rapture as His faithful servants, and some of the things to watch for as the time grows near.

> *...behold, I come quickly; and my reward is with me, to give every man according as his work shall be*   Revelation 22:12

In Matthew 24, Christ revealed what would take place over the entire *church age* without divulging that this would be a time when Christ would offer salvation and eternal life to Jews and Gentiles alike. When Christ delivered the *Olivet Discourse*, the Jews had been exclusively chosen by God for almost 2000 years, starting when Abraham was called into Canaan to birth a new nation. This came to an end when Jesus Christ initiated a New Covenant with both Jews and Gentiles.

The New Covenant (Age of Faith and Grace) will end at the Battle of Armageddon. After his 2nd advent, Christ will gather before Him people who have survived the Great Tribulation. He will then judge people from all nations of the world (Matthew 25: 31-32), He will use His *Rod of Iron* to separate the people into two groups (Ezekiel 20:37).

[33] *As I live, saith the Lord GOD, surely with a mighty hand, and with a stretched out arm, and with fury poured out, will I rule over you:*
[34] *And I will bring you out from the people, and will gather you out of the countries wherein ye are scattered, with a mighty hand, and with a stretched out arm, and with fury poured out.*
[35] *And I will bring you into the wilderness of the people, and there will I plead with you face to face.*
[36] *Like as I pleaded with your fathers in the wilderness of the land of Egypt, so will I plead with you, saith the Lord GOD.*
[37] *And I will cause you to pass under the rod, and I will bring you into the bond of the covenant:*
[38] *And I will purge out from among you the rebels, and them that transgress against me:* **I will bring them forth out of the country where they sojourn***, and they shall not enter into the land of Israel: and ye shall know that I am the LORD*   Ezekial 20: 33-38

The people of the nations will be separated into two groups: *Sheep* and *Goats*. The Sheep will be placed on His *right* and the Goats on His *left* (Matthew 25:34, Matthew 25:41). The sheep on Jesus' right hand are blessed by God the Father and will Join the Jews in the Land of Promise. The reason is stated:

For I was hungry and you gave me something to eat, I was thirsty and you gave me something to drink, I was a stranger and you invited me in, I needed clothes and you clothed me, I was sick and you looked after me, I was in prison and you came to visit me (Matthew 25: 35-36).

The righteous Sheep were *stunned* and did not understand:

> *[37] Lord, when did we see you hungry, and fed you? or thirsty, and gave you drink?*
> *[38] When did we see you a stranger, and take you in? or naked, and clothe you?*
> *[39] Or when did we see you sick, or in prison, and came unto you?*
> Matthew 25: 37-39

The King replied:

> *Verily I say unto you, inasmuch as ye have done it unto one of the least of these my brethren, ye have done it unto me*   Matthew 25:40

Who are these brethren? The question as to who are these brethren is easily answered. Jesus tells us in Matthew 12:50 that anyone who does the will of His Father is a *brother*. The same Greek word *(adelphos)* is translated as brother in Matthew 12:50, but is translated *brethren* in Matthew 25:40 and in Romans 8: 29-30. The symbolic meaning of the term *brethren* in the Bible cannot be overstated. In the Old Testament, it is used to denote the special relationship between brothers and sisters of the same parentage, and between members of the same culture. In the New Testament, it is used to signify the spiritual bond between believers in Christ. This timeless concept is still applicable today, making this a powerful and meaningful word with great impact even outside of religious contexts (Marcos Reyna). The *brethren* cannot be limited to both Jews and Gentiles that will join the 12 tribes in the Millennial Kingdom. The use of *adelphos* demands no such limitation. The brethren are both Jews and Gentiles that have been persecuted during the Great Tribulation.

It is usually concluded that this Parable reveals how all Christians should love and treat Israel. Not only Israel, but all people who are less fortunate than we are, and God will judge everyone as to how they responded. We are to love and care for strangers just as Christ did during His earthly ministry. This is all *absolutely true*, but this is the part of the Judgment of the Sheep and Goats that is easy to understand. The fundamental and basic tenet of the Christian religion is that salvation and eternal life are offered by faith as a *free gift* to all who accept Jesus Christ as Lord and Savior. Anything else is *works* and *obedience* to His commands. Good deeds do not determine salvation, but will be rewarded when we stand at the *Bema Seat Judgment* (II Corinthians 5:10, Romans 14:10). The Bema Seat Judgment is a man-made term and does not appear in the Holy Scriptures. It is derived from the old Roman Empire Olympic Games where men engaged in a race. The Bema Seat was a judgment seat which was at the finish line to determine the order of finish. Rewards of wreaths and medals were given to participants according to their rank. All modern track meets continue this ancient practice. The Bema Seat Judgment is not a judgment of condemnation, but for rewards of faithful service to all whose names are found in the Book of Life. No one can buy either eternal life or eternal rewards… these are gifts based upon *faith and service*. Good works cannot buy anyone salvation and eternal life. The Bible specifically tells us that we can only be saved by grace through our faith in Jesus Christ. This is not what happened in the Judgment of the Sheep and Goats.

To those on His right (Sheep):

> [34] Then shall the King say unto them on his right hand, Come, ye blessed of my Father, inherit the kingdom prepared for you from the foundation of the world:
> [35] For I was an hungry, and ye gave me meat: I was thirsty, and ye gave me drink: I was a stranger, and ye took me in:
> [36] Naked, and ye clothed me: I was sick, and ye visited me: I was in prison, and ye came unto me   Matthew 25: 34-36

To those on His left (Goats)

> **[41]** Then shall he say also unto them on the left hand, Depart from me, ye cursed, into everlasting fire, prepared for the devil and his angels:
> **[42]** For I was an hungry, and ye gave me no meat: I was thirsty, and ye gave me no drink:
> **[43]** I was a stranger, and ye took me not in: naked, and ye clothed me not: sick, and in prison, and ye visited me not   Matthew 25: 41-43

> And these shall go away into everlasting punishment: but the righteous into life eternal   Matthew 25:46

The paradox and problem are that salvation and eternal life is determined on how the Sheep *treated His brethren.* There is no mention whatsoever of faith or grace. Those that treated His brethren (Matthew 25:40) with mercy, respect, and generosity (The Sheep) were allowed to enter the 1000 Year Millennial Kingdom, and those who did not (The Goats) were condemned to the *Lake of Burning Fire* (Matthew 25:46).

The goats on the left hand of Jesus are cursed with eternal hell-fire, *prepared for the devil and his angels.* The reason is given: *They had the opportunity to minister to the Lord, but they did nothing* (Matthew 25: 42-43). The damned asked: *Lord, when did we see you hungry or thirsty or a stranger or needing clothes or sick or in prison, and did not help you?* (Matthew 25:44). Jesus replied: *I tell you the truth, whatever you did not do for one of the least of these, you did not do for me* (Matthew 25:45). Jesus then ends the discourse by repeating Matthew 25:41: *These* (those on His left) *shall go away into everlasting punishment: but the righteous* (those on His right) *into life eternal* (Matthew 25:46).

We are reminded what Jesus said to Saul of Tarsus when He appeared to him on the Road to Damascus: *Saul, Saul, why persecutest thou me?* (Acts 9:4). When Christ said this to Saul, He had been dead for several months, yet He accused Saul of persecuting Him personally! Imagine that!! When we as Christians are persecuted or afflicted by Satan and unbelievers, Christ knows and He suffers also!!! What an awesome, loving, and caring King we serve.

In this Parable, Jesus is judging two classes of people: those who will be redeemed and enter the Millennial Kingdom, and those who will be condemned and lost. Any reading of the parable seems to suggest that salvation is the result of *good works*. The *sheep* acted charitably, giving food, drink, and clothing to the needy. The *goats* showed no pity or help for those in need. This resulted in salvation for the sheep and damnation for the goats.

However, Scripture cannot contradict itself, and the Bible clearly and repeatedly teaches that salvation is by *faith* through the grace of God and *not* by our good works (John 1:12, Acts 15:11, Romans 3: 22-24, Romans 4: 4-8, Romans 7: 24-25, Romans 8:12, Galatians 3: 6-9, Ephesians 2: 8-10). It appears that the fate of those that are judged is determined by *works*……. The way that the *people of the nations* responded to the *brethren* of Christ and how they treated them when they were sick, hungry and in need. Under the *New Covenant*, it is clear that people are not saved by how they treat other people. In the *Age of Grace* (Church age) good deeds can never save anyone. We are repeatedly told that under the New Covenant: *By the deeds of the law there shall be no flesh justified* (Romans 3:20, Galatians 2:16). Salvation is: *Not of works lest any man can boast* (Ephesians 2:9).

The *Judgment of the Sheep and Goats* is very mysterious, not because of what it *does* teach but because of what it *does not* teach. There is no mention of faith and grace as a way to salvation, or Jesus Christ as the Jewish Messiah, or Christ as the source of salvation by faith under the New Covenant. There is a possible explanation:

As previously stated, it is clear that good deeds and charitable works cannot save anyone, but the words of Jesus Christ mention nothing about faith or spiritual rebirth. *How can this be explained?* It cannot, unless one accepts and studies the Bible as a dispensational document. The entire scriptural record of the Judgment of the Nations is in the 7th and last dispensation…the 1000-year Millennial Kingdom. This Judgment will take place to decide who will join the 144,000 sealed Jews (Revelation 7) in the Kingdom, and it will take place when Jesus Christ is seated on His *Throne of Glory* (Matthew 25:31). This entire scenario takes place *after* the Church age has ended. The *Dispensation of Grace* and salvation by *faith* is over when Christ assumes His rightful place as *King of Kings* on His *Throne of Glory*. The entire Body of Christ has been completed and joined Christ as His eternal bride at the rapture of all (alive or dead) believers (Revelation 19). Failure to understand how the eternal fate of those judged was determined is caused by the mistake of placing Matthew 25: 31-46 into the wrong dispensation, and then trying to explain it.

Explanation of the Judgment of the Nations is similar to one of the problems today in that Christians living in the *Dispensation of Grace* are still trying to live under the *Dispensation of the Law*. Preachers tell their congregation that if they do not tithe, they will be cursed: If a Catholic deliberately skips mass or Sunday services it is a sin: and if a Christian does not come to an alter call and ask for forgiveness of sins then they will be condemned forever. All of this…and more…is trying to live one's life in the Age of Grace by following the commands of God under the Old Covenant. Such teachings are heretic and fail to place the promises of God into their proper dispensation. This is the mistake that biblical scholars make when they try to explain the Judgment of the Nations by placing it under a set of rules and laws that no longer exist when Jesus Christ executes the Judgment of the Sheep and Goats. As previously stated, the sole criteria used to allow the Gentiles who are still alive after the Battle of Armageddon has been fought, and the Church Age (Dispensation of Grace) is over, is how they treated God's chosen people… primarily the Jews.

Think about *how* Jesus Christ separated those who are judged into two separate groups. Both the *Sheep* and the *Goats* will be judged by how they treated the *brethren* (The Jews) in their time of need, and the *Sheep* will be rewarded by participating in the blessings and rewards in the earthly 1000-year Millennial Kingdom; which God has reserved for the Jews since His covenant with Abraham. The *Goats* will be condemned to eternal punishment in the Lake of Burning Fire for failure to help God's chosen people. This New Dispensation will have different rules and rewards than that which preceded it...or it would not be a new dispensation.

The Seven Dispensations of Time
Matthew 25: 31-46 cannot possibly be explained or interpreted unless it is recognized that the entire bible is a *Dispensational Document* (Phillips, *The Eternal Plan of God)*. From when Adam was created to when the earth is purged of all sin, there are 7 distinct and different *dispensations*. A dispensation is a period of time during which God is dealing with His creations called earth and man in a distinct and different way. We are currently living in the 6th dispensation of time called the *Church Age*. The 5th dispensation of time was the *Age of the Law,* and the 7th dispensation of time will be the 1000-year *Millennial Kingdom*. Dispensational Bible Study is: *Study to shew thyself approved unto God…...rightly dividing the word of truth* (II Timothy 2:15), and placing each scripture into its proper dispensation. This is graphically displayed in a *Dispensational Diagram* shown on the next page, which was originally developed by that great dispensationalist Richard Jordan. The original diagram by Jordan has been modified to illustrate a new Pre-Wrath Rapture (Phillips, *A New Pre-Wrath Rapture Theory*). The 70th Week of Daniel is shown shaded in *Pink*.

The 6th *Dispensation of Faith and Grace*. (*Yellow* shading*)* will end at the Battle of Armageddon. When Jesus Christ returns to earth in His 2nd Advent, He will quickly defeat Satan and all of his demonic forces. The

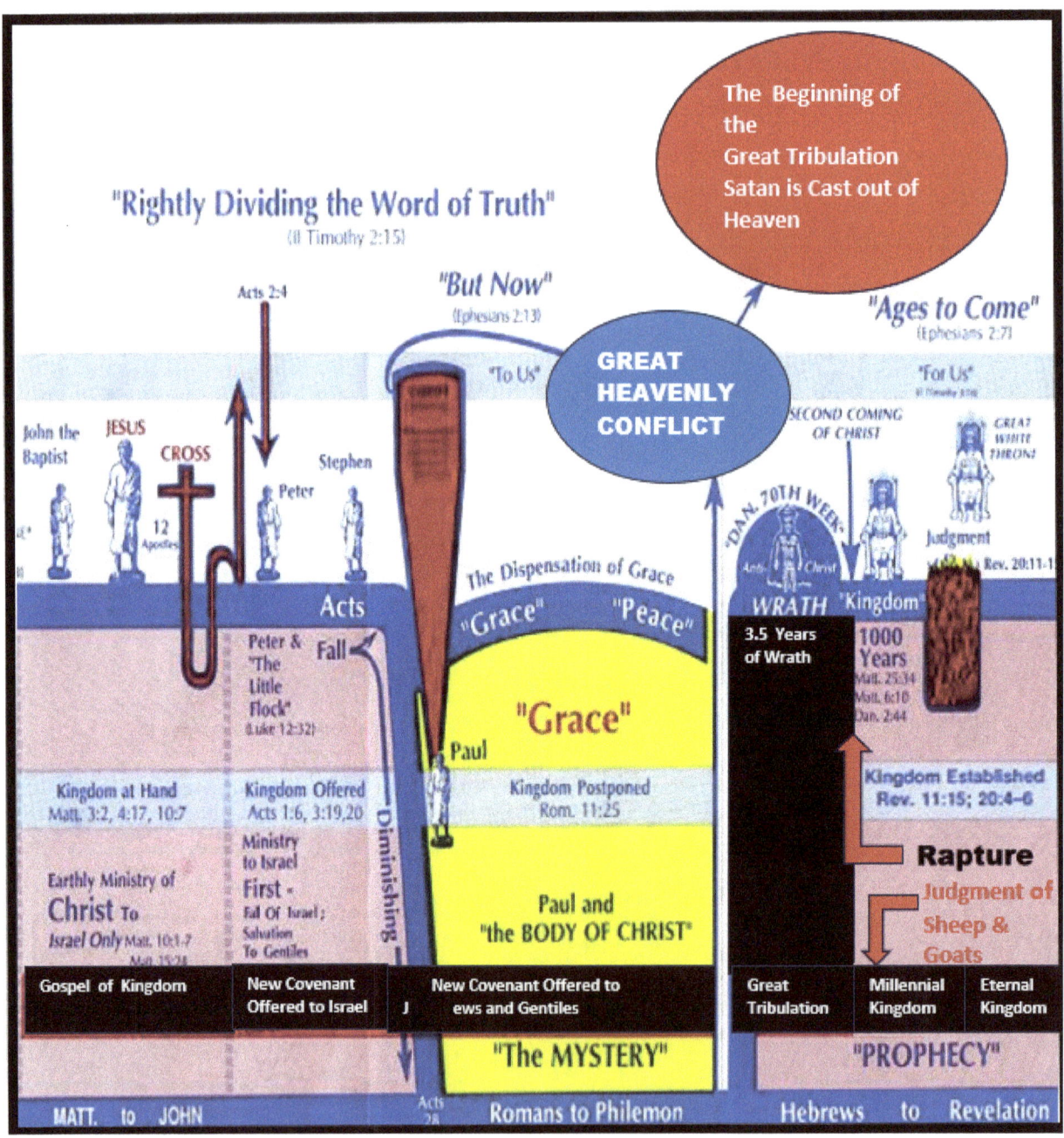

Antichrist and the False Prophet will be cast into the Lake of Burning Fire (Revelation 19:20), and all unbelievers will be incarcerated in a place called *Torments* where they will be held until the final White Throne Judgment. Satan will be bound in chains and thrown into the Bottomless Pit where he will remain for 1000 years (Revelation 20: 1-2).

The 7th and last Dispensation will be the *1000-Year Millennial Kingdom*. It will end with the *Great White Throne Judgment*. The *Judgment of the Sheep and Goats* is likely to occur just before or after the Jewish Feast of Tabernacles (Tishri 15); either just before the Millennial Kingdom begins are just as it is beginning. The scriptures do not say exactly when it will take place, but it is *not* in the *Age of Grace.*

The Dispensation of Grace was completely unknown to all of the Old Testament prophets: It was called a *Mystery* by Paul until He revealed it. The last 7 years of Daniel's 70th Week began when Christ was baptized by John at the River Jordan. The 3.5-year ministry of Christ *must* be included in the 70th and last week of Daniel because the entire prophecy is Jewish, and Christ entire ministry was to the Jews (Phillips, *The Daniel 70 Week Prophecy: The Cornerstone of Biblical Prophecy*).

The 3.5 years of Christ's *Ministry of Reconciliation* were documented in the Books of Matthew, Mark, Luke, and John in the Holy Bible. The last 3.5 years of Daniels 70th and final week are described by Christ in the *Olivet Discourse* and in the Book of Revelation. This is Daniel's 70th Week.

The entire 1000-year Millennial Kingdom is a fulfillment of God's *Covenant* with Abraham, Moses, and King David that one day the *Land of Promise* (Genesis 12: 18-21, Genesis 26:3) will be allocated to 12 tribes of Israel.

It is within this setting and context that we must understand and interpret the *Judgment of the Nations (Sheep and Goats Judgment)*.

The 2nd Advent of Jesus Christ will be in two parts. The **1st** will be when He returns in the air to gather all true believers…. alive and dead….to meet Him in the air. This is the *rapture* or resurrection of all the *ecclesia*. The **2nd** will be when Jesus Christ returns to earth to fight the Battle of Armageddon. The *Wedding of the Lamb* will take place in heaven following the rapture of the Church. It is conjectured that the *Battle of*

Armageddon will be fought on the *Feast of Yom Kippur*, 10 days after the Jewish Feast of Trumpets. The *Wedding Supper* will be held on the Jewish *Feast of Tabernacles*, 5 days after the Battle of Armageddon (Phillips, *The 7 Feasts of Israel*). *The Bema Seat Judgment* of all believers (for rewards) will immediately take place between the Battle of Armageddon (Tishri 10) and the Feast of Tabernacles (Tishri 15-21). The Church age and the last half of Daniel's 70th Week will both end on *Yom Kippur*. It is not clear from scripture exactly when the *Judgment of the Sheep and Goats* will take place, but we know for certain that Christ will judge the people of the Nations from His Throne of Glory (Matthew 25:31).

Since Christ will be seated on His Millennial Throne, we know that the Judgment of the Nations will take place in the initial stages of the 7th and last dispensation. He will likely Judge the Nations on a high plateau just north of Jerusalem (Micah 4: 1-2). This judgment should not be confused with the *Great White Throne Judgment* which will be held after the 1000-year Millennial Kingdom. This is a judgment which belongs in the Millennial Kingdom and not in the Age of Grace

Those who will pass under the *rod of judgment* and are placed on the right-hand-side of Jesus Christ (Sheep) will enter into the Millennial Kingdom: Those who are placed upon the Left-hand-side of Christ (Goats) will be condemned to eternal punishment in the *Lake of Burning Fire* (Matthew 25:46). Those who enter into the Millennial Kingdom will have earned that right by how they treated the breteren, particularly the Jews. The purpose of the *Judgment of the Nations* (Sheep and Goats) is to *determine who will enter into the Millennial Kingdom*. They will be accompanied by *the 144,000 sealed Jews from 12 tribes of Israel* (Revelation 7: 1-8). Note once again that the Church age (Age of Grace) has ended. The Body of Christ has a *heavenly calling* and the Jews have an *earthly calling*.

Regardless of when the rapture takes place (Pre-Tribulation Rapture, Mid-Tribulation Rapture, Classic Pre-Wrath Rapture, or the new Pre-Wrath Rapture proposed by (Phillips, A New Pre-Wrath Rapture Theory): Many Christians will be martyred for their faith during the Wrath of Satan, but many will survive both the Wrath of Satan and the Wrath of God. These Christians (Jews and Gentiles) in Israel and in Europe will be persecuted the most. Some who live on other continents and remote locations… including the fleeing remnant of Israel who will hide in the Wilderness of Judea (Matthew 24:15-16, Matthew 25:32, Isaiah 63, Revelation 12: 14, 17) will also be persecuted by Satan, and his demons, but to a lesser degree. Scripture indicates that this will be a difficult time for the Jews. There will many Jews and Gentiles who have been blessed with resources that they will share with the Jews.

For I was hungry, and you gave me food: I was thirsty and you gave me drink: I was naked and you gave me clothes: I was in prison and you comforted me

The *Great White Throne Judgment* is to judge the unrighteous dead and sentence them to the Lake of Burning Fire. Note that The Sheep and Goats Judgment is to determine which *Jews* and *Gentiles*… and *Foolish Virgins*… will enter into the Millennial Kingdom. The diagram on the next page illustrates who will be at the Sheep & Goats Judgment.

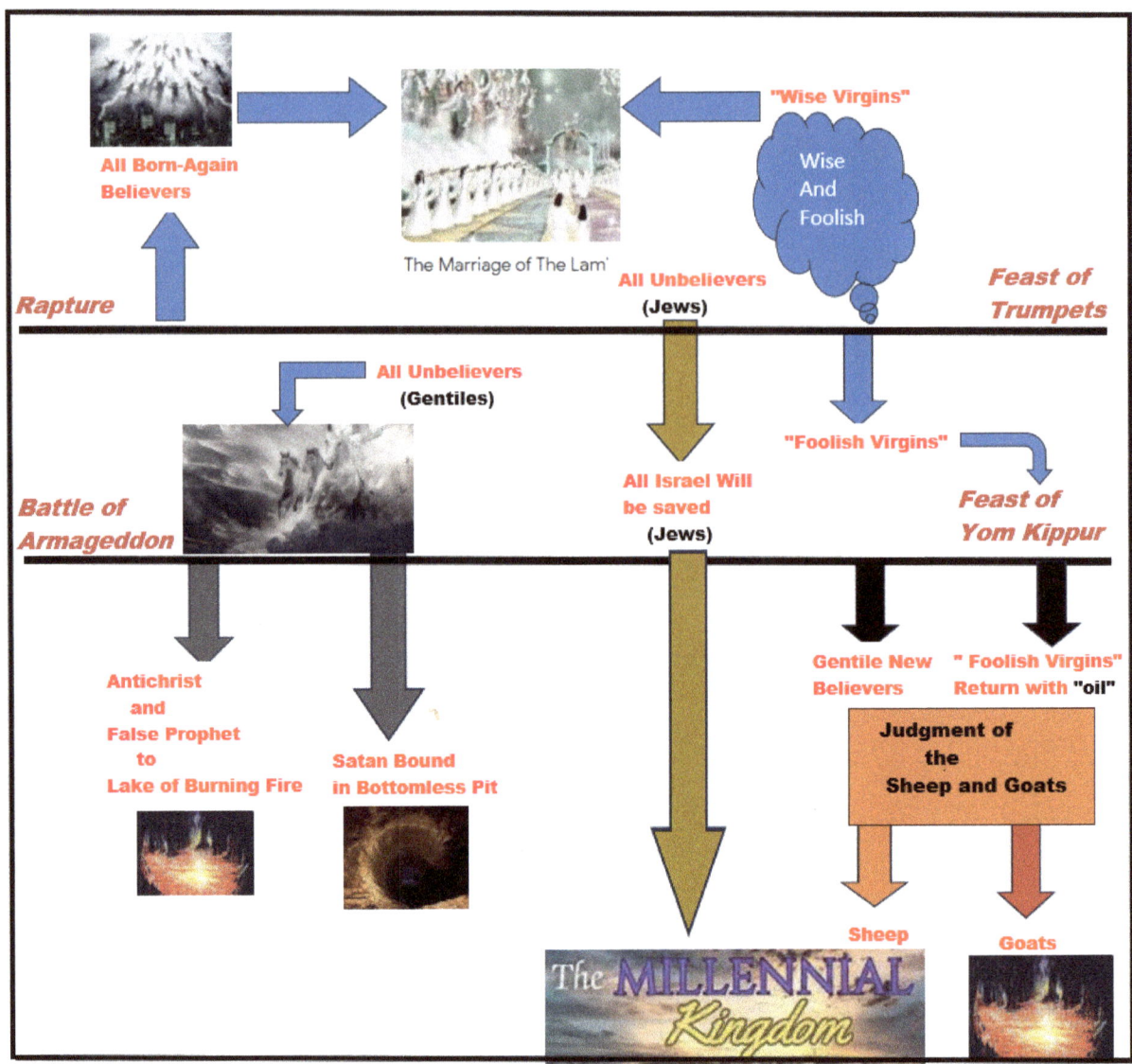

The Judgment of the Nations is based upon how the *Sheep* treated the Jews during the Great Tribulation. The judgment is based only on *works*. The only way that the Judgment of the Sheep and Goats can be explained is that it ***does not*** apply to the Church Age of Faith and Grace. It takes place in the *Millennial Kingdom after* the church age is over, and just as one cannot take the Laws in the 5th Dispensation and apply it to the 6th Dispensation, which is the Age of Grace….one cannot apply the rules of the 6th Dispensation (Church Age) to the 7th and last dispensation; the 1000-year Millennial Kingdom. The people who are being judged are those Jews, Gentiles and the Foolish Virgins who found oil (Holy Spirit) after the rapture. All of these individuals have survived in the nations of the world during what Jesus called *The Great Tribulation* (Matthew 24:21).

Immediately following the rapture of all the ecclesia, there will be no born-again believers upon the face of the earth. The *Wise Virgins* will be taken to Heaven with Christ to become His Bride. The *Foolish Virgins*, and those unbelieving Jews and Gentiles who survive the Great Tribulation and remain in the Nations of the World, will be gathered together and judged by Jesus Christ from His Throne of Glory. After the Battle of Armageddon, there will be no unbelievers upon the face of the earth and *all of Israel* (those alive) *will be saved* (Romans 11: 25-26).

Those who pass under the *Rod* of Christ Judgment and placed upon His right will enter into the Millennial Kingdom. It is my belief that the 144,000 Jews who are sealed in Revelation 7: 1-8 will also enter the Millennial Kingdom and inherit the land. They will not be raptured out, but they are sealed from the Wrath of God to protect them and survive the 7 Bowl Judgments of God (Revelation 7: 1-8, Revelation 15:1, Revelation 16:1). All will have accepted Christ as their long-awaited Messiah.

> ***Authors Comment***: Notice that the sealing of the 144,000 in Revelation 7 1-8 is immediately followed by a description of *a great multitude, which no man could number, of all nations, and kindreds, and people, and tongues, stood before the throne, and before the Lamb, clothed with white robes, and palms in their hands* (Revelation 7:9). This great multitude which no man can number is identical to the number described in Revelation 11: 18. This is without a doubt those who are taken away in the rapture. Notice that the sealing of the 144,000 and the multitude that no man can number in Revelation 7:9 both occur together. This is a strong indication that both the sealing of the 144,000

and the rapture occur at the same point in time; when the 7th Trumpet sounds (Phillips, *A New Pre-Wrath Rapture Theory*)

It is appropriate to explain one of the main things that is expected of those individuals who will enter the Millennial Kingdom.

*[16] And it shall come to pass, that **every one that is left of all the nations** which came against Jerusalem shall even go up from year to year to worship the King, the LORD of hosts, and to **keep the feast of tabernacles.***
[17] And it shall be, that whoso will not come up of all the families of the earth unto Jerusalem to worship the King, the LORD of hosts, even upon them shall be no rain.
[18] And if the family of Egypt go not up, and come not, that have no rain; there shall be the plague, wherewith the LORD will smite the heathen that come not up to keep the Feast of Tabernacles.
[19] This shall be the punishment of Egypt, and the punishment of all nations that come not up to keep the Feast of Tabernacles
Zachariah 14: 16-19

The *Feast of Tabernacles* is the 7th and last of the *7 Feasts of Israel* which were ordained by God during the Exodus from Egypt (Phillips, *The 7 Feasts of Israel*). During the 1000-year Millennial Kingdom *all nations of the world* will be required to attend the 8-day Feast of Tabernacles every year in Jerusalem (Zachariah 14:16,19). It is *mandatory* that a delegation from every nation throughout the world attend this festival. Failure to comply to this commandment will result in *no rain* during the next year and a *plague* upon the people (Zachariah 14:18). Again, this is not a New Covenant command, but instructions about what the people of every nation will be forced to do in the Millennial Kingdom. The original inhabitants of the Kingdom will multiply and spread across the world during the 1000-year Millennial Kingdom.

Finally, the 144,000, and a believing remnant of Jews and Gentiles (Sheep), will both enter the kingdom in their mortal bodies. They will all live long lives as before the Great Flood, and they will procreate and populate the kingdom (Isaiah 65:20), but not all their children will become believers. The *unbelievers* from the 1000-year Millennial Kingdom will join Satan at the end of the 1000-years when he is released from the *Bottomless Pit*. They will all gather to assault Jerusalem and the Throne of Jesus Christ. At this point in time, *God Himself* will appear and immediately eradicate all rebels and all rebellion with fire from heaven (Revelation 20:9). The earth will at that time be purged of *all* non-believers and the *Great White Throne Judgement* will take place (Revelation 20:11-15). The earth will be cleansed and renovated by fire, and the Messianic Kingdom will merge into God's eternal kingdom (I Corinthians 15: 24-28).

[1] *And I saw a new heaven and a new earth: for the first heaven and the first earth were passed away; and there was no more sea.*
[2] *And I John saw the holy city, new Jerusalem, coming down from God out of heaven, prepared as a bride adorned for her husband.*
[3] *And I heard a great voice out of heaven saying, Behold, the tabernacle of God is with men, and he will dwell with them, and they shall be his people, and God himself shall be with them, and be their God.*
[4] *And God shall wipe away all tears from their eyes; and there shall be no more death, neither sorrow, nor crying, neither shall there be any more pain: for the former things are passed away.*
[5] *And he that sat upon the throne said, Behold, I make all things new. And he said unto me: Write: for these words are true and faithful.*
[6] *And he said unto me: It is done. I am Alpha and Omega, the beginning and the end. I will give unto him that is athirst of the fountain of the water of life freely.*
[7] *He that overcometh shall inherit all things; and I will be his God, and he shall be my son.*   Revelation 21: 1-7

EPILOG

The words of Jesus Christ are often difficult to understand because His wisdom and insight is so far above human intellectual capacity. The *Parable of the Sheep and Goats* is a prime example of this observation. As previously stated, at *face value* this parable seems to teach that salvation is dependent upon *works*. Such a conclusion violates the basic tenet of Christian doctrine. Salvation is obtained by *faith* and faith alone, and it is appropriated by *grace. So, what is faith?*

...we look not at the things which are seen, but at the things which are not seen: for the things which are seen are temporal; but the things which are not seen are eternal   II Corinthians 4:18

... faith is the substance of things hoped for, the evidence of things not seen   Hebrews 11:1

... without faith it is impossible to please God   Hebrews 11:6

Faith cannot be seen and it cannot be measured. It is fundamental to being a Christian, but we cannot fully understand it. It is like the air that we breath; we know that it is necessary for us to live as Born-again Christians, but it cannot be seen.

Suppose that Christ in the Parable of the Sheep and Goats was not teaching the substance of works, but He was teaching His disciples how to *recognize* a true Christian? *How can a Christian be recognized*? Does a Born-again Christian turn blue or wear priestly garments? No…. but a Christian is clearly recognized by what they do and speak.

Knowing that a man is not justified by the works of the law, but by the faith of Jesus Christ, even we have believed in Jesus Christ, that we might be justified by the faith of Christ, and not by the works of the law: for by the works of the law shall no flesh be justified   Galatians 2:16

[17] Even so faith, if it hath not works, is dead, being alone.

[18] *Yea, a man may say: Thou hast faith, and I have works: shew me thy faith without thy works, and I will shew thee my faith by my works*
James 2: 17-18

Works are the physical manifestation of *faith*. The New Testament is perfectly clear in many places that faith is expressed by works.

His brethren therefore said unto him: Depart hence, and go into Judaea, that thy disciples also may see the works that thou doest   John 7:3

Jesus answered them, I told you, and ye believed not: the works that I do in my Father's name, they bear witness of me.   John 10:25

Verily, verily, I say unto you, He that believeth on me, the works that I do shall he do also; and greater works than these shall he do; because I go unto my Father.   John 14:12

[14] *Every man's work shall be made manifest: for the day shall declare it, because it shall be revealed by fire; and the fire shall try every man's work of what sort it is.*
[15] *If any man's work abides which he hath built thereupon, he shall receive a reward.*   I Corinthians 3: 14-15

Therefore, my beloved brethren, be ye steadfast, unmovable, always abounding in the work of the Lord, forasmuch as ye know that your labor is not in vain in the Lord   I Corinthians 15:58

There is something about a born-again Christian that the world cannot understand. A true Christian will: *Love your enemies, bless them that curse you, do good to them that hate you, and pray for them which despitefully use you, and persecute you* (Matthew 5:44). The world can never understand or conform to these commands. God has equipped every Born-again Christian to live by these standards. He has given us the Holy Spirit to be Christ-like in the face of adversity and oppression.

Bibliography

Coulter, Fred R., The Appointed Times of Jesus the Messiah, York Publishing Company, PO Box 1038, Hollister, California, 95024-1038

Coulter, Fred R., The Day That Jesus the Christ Died, York Publishing Company, PO Box 1038, Hollister, California, 95024-1038

Dake, Finis J., Dake's Annotated Reference Bible, Dake Bible Sales, P.O. Box 1050, Lawrenceville, Ga., 30246

Finegan, Jack, Handbook of Biblical Chronology, Hendrickson Publishing Company, Peabody, Ma.

Good, Joseph, Rosh Hashanah and the Messianic Kingdom to Come, Hatikva Ministries, PO Box 3125, Port Arthur, Texas 77643-0703

Horn H. S. and L. H. Wood, The Chronology of Ezra, TEACH Services, Inc., www.teachservices.com

Larkin, Clarence, Dispensational Truth, P.O. Box 334, Glenside, Pa., 1920

Logos apostolic Church of God and Bible College, Interlinear Greek and Hebrew Translation, Logos apostolic.org, United Kingdom, Logos apostolic.org

Nee, Watchman, Come Lord Jesus, Christian Fellowship Publishers, Inc., 11515 Allecingie Parkway, Richmond, Virginia 23235

Phillips, Don T., The Book of Revelation: *Mysteries Revealed*, 2nd Edition, Virtual Bookworm. com, PO Box 9949, College Station, Tx 77845

Phillips, Don T., The Book of Ruth: *Historical and Prophetic Truths*, Virtual Bookworm. com, PO Box 9949, College Station, Tx, 77845

Phillips, Don T., Life After Death: *Mysteries Revealed*, Virtual Bookworm. com, PO Box 9949, College Station, Tx, 77845

Phillips, Don T., The Eternal Plan of God: *Dispensations, Covenant Promises, Salvation*, Virtual Bookworm. com, PO Box 9949, College Station, Texas 7784.

Phillips, Don T., *The Birth and Death of Christ*, Virtual Bookworm. com, PO Box 9949, College Station, Tx, 77845

Phillips, Don T., The Book of Exodus: *Historical and Prophetic Truths* Virtual Bookworm. com, PO Box 9949, College Station, Tx, 77845

Phillips, Don T., A Biblical Chronology from Adam to Christ, Virtual Bookworm. com, PO Box 9949, College Station, Tx, 77845

Phillips, Don T., Life After the Great Tribulation: *The Millennial Kingdom,* Virtual Bookworm. com, PO Box 9949, College Station, Tx, 77845

Phillips, Don T., The Last 50 Days of Jesus Christ Virtual Bookworm. com, PO Box 9949, College Station, Tx, 77845

Phillips, Don T., The Daniel 70 Week Prophecy Virtual Bookworm. com, PO Box 9949, College Station, Texas 77845

Phillips, Don T., The Day of the Lord Virtual Bookworm. com, PO Box 9949, College Station, Texas 77845

Phillips, Don T., The Birth of Christ: *A Forensic Analysis of the Birth of Jesus Christ*

Virtual Bookworm. com, PO Box 9949, College Station, Tx, 77845

Phillips, Don T., The Wrath and Judgments of God
Virtual Bookworm. com, PO Box 9949, College Station, Texas 77845

Phillips, Don T., Biblical Truths about Difficult Concepts
Virtual Bookworm. com, PO Box 9949, College Station, Texas 77845

Phillips, Don T., A New Pre-Wrath Rapture Theory
Virtual Bookworm. com, PO Box 9949, College Station, Texas 77845

Phillips, Don T., Rapture and Resurrection: The Blessed Hope of All Believers, Virtual Bookworm. com, PO Box 9949, College Station, Texas   77845

Phillips, Don T., The 7 Feasts of Israel, Virtual Bookworm. com, PO Box 9949, College Station, Texas   7784

Rosenthal, Matthew, The Pre-Wrath Rapture of the Church, Thomas Nelson Publishers, Nashville, Tennessee

Ryrie, Charles C., The Ryrie Study Bible, King James Version, Moody Press, Chicago. Ill

Salerno, Donald A., Revelation Unsealed, Virtual Bookworm.Com, P.O. Box 9949, College Station, Texas, 77842

Thiele, Edwin R., The Mysterious Numbers of the Hebrew Kings: *Revised Edition*, Kregel, Grand Rapids, Michigan

Thomas, Robert L., Revelation 1-7, An Exegetical Commentary, Moody Press, Chicago, Illinois

Thomas, Robert L., Revelation 8-22, An Exegetical Commentary, Moody Press, Chicago, Illinois

Van Kampen, Robert, The Sign, Crossway Books, 1300 Crescent Street, Wheaton, Illinois 60187

Walvoord, John F., The Millennial Kingdom, Academic Books, Zondervan Publishing Company, 1415 Lake Drive S.E., Grand Rapids, Michigan 49506

Footnote: This manuscript has drawn upon several excellent websites found by GOOGLE search. It is my intention to recognize every biblical scholar and source of information from those *giants that walked before me*. This information was sometimes not made available. In other cases, information was marked open source or not marked at all. If any author(s) sees any material that they want referenced, please contact me and I will acknowledge their previous research and scholarly work. In any case, I am extremely grateful for previous investigations or conclusions that may (or may not) support this work. God will know them and He will know the source.

Don T. Phillips
Author
phillipsdon60@gmail.com

Spring, 2024

www.ingramcontent.com/pod-product-compliance
Lightning Source LLC
Chambersburg PA
CBHW060950170426
43202CB00026B/2999